All Faces but Mine

Middle East Literature in Translation
Michael Beard and Adnan Haydar, *Series Editors*

KING FAHD CENTER FOR MIDDLE EAST STUDIES

**TRANSLATION OF ARABIC LITERATURE
2013 AWARD WINNER**

Syracuse University Press and the King Fahd Center for Middle East and Islamic Studies, University of Arkansas, are pleased to announce ALL FACES BUT MINE *as the 2014 co-winner of the King Fahd Center for Middle East Studies Translation of Arabic Literature Award.*

All
Faces but
Mine

THE POETRY OF SAMIH AL-QASIM

Translated from the Arabic by Abdulwahid Lu'lu'a

SYRACUSE UNIVERSITY PRESS

Syracuse University Press
Syracuse, New York 13244-5290

All Rights Reserved

First Edition 2015

15 16 17 18 19 20   6 5 4 3 2 1

For a listing of books published and distributed by Syracuse University Press,
visit https://press.syr.edu.

ISBN: 978-0-8156-1052-6 (paperback)   978-0-8156-5328-8 (e-book)

Library of Congress Cataloging-in-Publication Data

Qasim, Samih.
[Poems. Selections. English]
All faces but mine : the poetry of Samih al-Qasim / translated from the Arabic
by Abdulwahid Lu'lu'a. — First edition.
pages cm
Includes bibliographical references and index.
ISBN 978-0-8156-1052-6 (pbk. : alk. paper) — ISBN 978-0-8156-5328-8 (e-book)
I. Lu'lu'ah, 'Abd al-Wahid, translator.   II. Title.
PJ7858.A78A2 2015
892.7'16—dc23   2015032246

CONTENTS

INTRODUCTION

Arabic poetry in Palestine assumed its characteristic tone from about 1948, when it became highly expressive of defiance and resistance to the Israeli occupation of historic Palestine. That type of poetry, more and more liberated from the residues of romanticism and late nineteenth-century French sentimentalism, became involved with the new situation of the Palestinian, threatened in his homeland by aliens from all over Europe.

A significant figure was that of Abdulrahim Mahmood (1913–1948), later known as the Martyr Poet. As a young man in the village of Anabta, he received the visiting Saudi prince in 1935 with a poem that showed his real Palestinian mettle. He bluntly asked the future king of Saudi Arabia, "Have you come to visit the Aqsa Mosque, or to bid farewell before it is lost"? Later, as a graduate of the Military Academy in Baghdad, the poet joined the Palestinian forces fighting against foreign occupation and fell in the battle of *Alshajara* in 1948.

After the *Nakba* (catastrophe) of 1948, a number of poets in Palestine turned more frequently toward the urgent affair of liberation of the homeland from an increasingly entrenched foreign occupation. Two talented young poets emerged and were to dominate the poetry scene in Palestine throughout the twenty-first century: Samih Al-Qasim, who was born in 1939 and published his first collection of poetry in 1958 as the *Sun Processions*, when he was barely nineteen years old; and Mahmood Darwish (1941–2008), who published his first collection of poetry in 1960 as *Sparrows without Wings*, also when he was nineteen years old. Those two talented Palestinian poets had so much in common that they were described by critics as "the two halves of the orange." Mahmood published twenty-six collections of poems and nine works of prose of a highly poetic charge.

vii

His poetry has been translated into twenty-three languages. Samih published seventy-seven works between 1958 and 2013. Fifty-six of those are poetry, eighteen are prose works, and three are translations. Selections of Samih's poetry were translated into fourteen languages. Like his "other soul," Samih's prose has a high poetic charge, and the work of both poets focuses mainly on Palestinian and international topics of struggle for freedom and independence.

Interestingly, some readers cannot quite tell whether a certain poem belongs to Samih or to Mahmood if they are not alerted beforehand. This is a peculiar phenomenon in poetry that deserves special treatment. Resistance poetry attracted poets throughout the Arab lands to embrace the Palestinian cause. Even an eminent Arab love poet, Nizar Qabbani (1923–1998), was moved to write, "Now that I have a rifle, take me with you to Palestine, oh, freedom fighters." The poem was sung by the famous Egyptian and pan-Arab singer Um-Kalthoom, which consecrated Palestinian resistance poetry throughout the Arab world.

Samih's first two collections of poetry, the *Sun Processions* (1958) and *The Road Songs* (1964), antagonized Israeli occupation authorities, who charged the poet with "instigation to revolution" and "propagation of Nasserite ideology." He had been imprisoned and condemned to hard labor for refusing the Israeli law of 1956 to draft Durooz Arabs in the Israeli army. A curious punishment was to force Samih to work at the morgue of an Israeli hospital. Details of the poet's imprisonments and dismissals from various jobs are painfully described in his recent autobiography, *It's Just an Ashtray* (2011).

His collections of 1958 and 1964 were followed by two more in 1965 and 1967, always celebrating the revolution and resistance of occupation, making the poet and his work very popular in Palestine and the Arab world. His new collections came out practically every year, and all the Israeli authorities could do was more dismissals from jobs, more imprisonments and house arrests. The confiscation of his published poetry did not stop the poet from writing more in the same revolutionary vein. In 1969 Jean-Paul Sartre visited Israel, and he mediated with the authorities to release the collection *The Arrival of the Thunderbird*.

As early as Samih's third collection, *Iram* (1965), published when the poet was twenty-six years old, he developed a genre of poetry which he called *Sirbiyya*, flock poem. This is like a *sirb*, flock of birds that fly together but occasionally one or two birds move ahead of the flock, or move sideways or backwards for a while, only to rejoin the rest of the flock. Ideas or images may shoot out of the body of the poem to develop or augment a new image or idea, thus adding to the richness of the poem. There are twelve such "flock poems" among the fifty-six collections that the poet produced in his career. Especially attractive are *The Desert* (1984), *The Deserts Let Me Down* (1998), *Funeral Oration by the Deceased at His Memorial Celebration* (2000), *Atlantis King* (2003), and *I Regret* (2009).

Funeral Oration by the Deceased at His Memorial Celebration is a fifty-five-page-long flock poem where the dead-alive hero is the Palestinian, who is absent-present. This narrator addresses the Arab nations who are clever only in holding memorial days for the dead, showing their concern by bringing flowers, mostly artificial, "slow to wither," or sending condolence telegrams or telephone messages. The dead-alive hero identifies with Hamlet in his tragedy, where his uncle, the real criminal, the invader, has married Hamlet's mother, Palestine, the motherland of the poet. Like Hamlet, the Palestinian is bewildered between illusion—the image of his father, the phantom, the image of the Arab nations, gathered only to commemorate the dead—and reality, the invader who married the homeland, the hero's mother, and the supposed reality of the existence of the Arab nations. The situation is ironic beyond realization. Although delegations from far and wide have only contributed enough to supply a comfortable coffin, they expect all the gratitude of the deceased, who addresses them in language so sarcastic that it even leads to an apology to that woman whose makeup was disturbed by her tears! Trifles like the funeral celebration itself are what keep the "crowds" of the Arab states busy, but the marriage of the motherland to the uncle-invader has become fodder for historians and storytellers, without any real action taken to remedy this illegal marriage. Then one bird shoots out of the flock in the form of an image of "war that looked like war," not a real one, followed by "peace that looked like peace." Everything here is unlike what it is, like the live Palestinian who is unlike the dead one. Every now and then a bird let loose from the flock is an image of a compulsory link to the flock, and keeps the reader at his/her toes until they return to the flock.

The "Arab Hamlet" keeps on asking desperate questions: how can he believe the fog, the mythical marriage of the mother and the uncle? Where are you, my father/the Arabs? The stray bird returns to the flock to witness the "funeral banquet" and hear the "fly buzzing" of the Arab media and their elegies. The hero, bored with all these theatrical activities, turns inward to enjoy the "mirrors of the homeland," only to see "faces of all nations, except his own nation's faces." This leads to a "boring turning round," this "presence-absence," this everything that is unlike itself. In his desperation, the hero calls for death as a solution. But soon he resumes his optimism and hope for coming change. Yet his soul asks when and how that change will come, when around him "the people of life, the Arabs, are enjoying their banquets, dancing and singing, drunk, among graves."

Another stray bird shoots upwards, above the flock, and the hero sees in the fog, like the phantom of the father in the fog, Cavaliers galloping on horseback. But soon the fog clears up and no riders are seen. Empty promises, much ado about nothing. The only succor left is love. Hamlet was in love with Ophelia, but even that love failed. The hero was in love with his land. Now even that land failed him. Why? It is because the beautiful cannot love a prince without a scepter. The Palestinian has no power in his hand, no weapon. How can the Palestinian be without any power? To be or not to be, there remains the question. Because the prince has no power, the beautiful land/Ophelia became a prey for hunters, claiming they love her. But all those so-called lovers are men without chests. Ophelia-homeland has no chest but that of her prince, the Arabian Hamlet. Here we are snatched back to the festival masque of the beginning of the poem.

Atlantis King is another flock poem in allegorical style, tinted with Greek mythology, which makes the poem too abstruse for the casual reader, too full of direct address and clichéd nationalism for the lover of poetry. The only source of the Atlantis myth is what Plato learned from the ancient Egyptian monks about a great island bequeathed by Poseidon, the sea god, to Atlantis, whose five sons were all kings on that island. But when the divine element in those five kings was superseded by the human element they were punished by Zeus, and the island was sunk into the sea.

The poem is an allegory of the life and death of Yasir Arafat, King Atlantis, and his management or mismanagement of the kingdom of Palestine, which led to the tragic end. This is an oversimplification of the skeleton of the poem, which needs a thorough reading and patient contemplation to realize the meanings and significance of characters and events that inform the poem. The protagonist opens his drama with an ominous description. He sounds like a one-man chorus who sees what is going to happen. The very first lines put us on the edge of our seats in expectation of what could not be a happy ending, if not totally tragic. "On water stands my throne, and my kingdom, of water is my scepter subjects." How viable is a kingdom of water at the mercy of the sea? The retinue of the king is vapor. He is pledged allegiance by seaweed. This king is newly come to the world. He is not a Shahrayar, deeply versed in kingship, not trained in the ways of the world. Therefore his story cannot go on like that of Scheherazade. His story has no beginning, as it begins with its end. How is that possible except in a mythical allegorical world? But this is the world of Atlantis-Palestine.

The individual birds in the flock of this poem are more easily discernible when one bird flies off, so we can recognize it better, in the descriptions of the protagonist of the poem. These are obvious, made too familiar by the media to be missed for an image of King Yasir of Atlantis-Palestine. The mythical-allegorical atmosphere is variegated by the language of cinematography, circus, chess game, and colloquial Americanisms. That is a harsh reminder that we are in the here and now, not in the mythological world. The poet addresses the king bluntly: you have miscalculated, so you have to pay the price. And the water throne begins to sink. The king tells us from the beginning that he has prepared himself for the fire baptism and has ventured with his innocence. So he was not unrealistic. And more is the pity. All that is left for us is a tragic sympathy that does not go very far in this mad, mad world.

I Regret is the third flock poem that calls for some introductory notes. This is a poem of close to 140 pages that came out in 2009 as a reaction to

the Israeli bombardment of Gaza in 2008. The unusually ominous intro-
duction, reproducing a page from the Old Testament (Joshua 10:12–28)
informs the poem. In the 2008 bombardment of Gaza, present-day Israelis
behaved in the same manner of the ancient Israelites under the leadership
of Joshua. The two thought that God was fighting the Palestinians for
them when they defeated the five Palestinian kings and hurled them in
a cave, covering the mouth of the cave with a great rock, so they would
perish unnoticed. The poet, like Hamlet, is holding a mirror so the Israeli
can see in himself his real human nature, which is not different from the
basic nature of the Palestinian. The Palestinian addresses the Israeli as
"my friend and rich-poor enemy." Yes, that enemy is rich, but the difficult
life of the Palestinian is costly; so is his death. This is repeated several
times in the poem as an embarrassing question: why do you want to kill
me, my children and land, for such a high price? I regret, says the Pales-
tinian, that I was born naturally, not according to the financial system
which is all you know. I was born not to live but for you to sever my head.
Then the adamant decision roars: I will resist. This is the leitmotif of the
entire poem. Remember, says the Palestinian to the Israeli, remember that
I visited your mother's grave in the icy European weather, which could be
Poland, and laid flowers on her grave, like a good human being. I even
thought of reciting the *Fatihah Soora*, as I would do before a Muslim
grave. But you have learned nothing from your mother's death. It did not
teach you to feel and behave as a good human being. I regret that you are
what you are. The defiance takes the form of "You kill me in vain. I am
the surviving and lasting wisdom, I am the corner stone. My children will
defeat your fire and banner. I was born to live, and live, and live." To the
incessant questions to the Israeli, why do you want to kill me, which have
no answer, the Palestinian says, I know, your mind weeps and your heart
bleeds—I think that you are a human being. One bird shoots sideways
from the flock to introduce an image not too unconnected with the main
argument, showing the basic humanity of the Palestinian as he invites
his enemy-friend to a meal, though not kosher. The "heavy guest" had to
leave as the situation was not to his liking, to the regret of the Palestinian.
As soon as that bird resumes its flight with the flock, another bird shoots
forward to display the killing field, with remains of killed people, broken

toys of babies, a dinner table covered with dust, a walking stick of an old man. So, my enemy-friend, the narrator concludes, learn to say, "I regret."

A return to the details of oppression is temporarily relieved by another flight of a bird from the flock to present an image of the happy home life of the Israeli. The children of the enemy-friend play around the house of the Palestinian, who offers them his own food and cakes, treating them kindly, while the Israeli pours bullets on Palestinian children. The Palestinian reminds the Israeli of the time when the Jews were persecuted, burned alive in the civilized Catholic Spain of Ferdinand and Isabella. They could not find refuge except in Arab and Muslim lands.

The one-sided argument goes on, punctuated with individual birds introducing new ideas and images in an attempt to get any answer from the Israeli. But there is no use, as the Israeli can never say I regret. Yet the Palestinian is always defiant and intent upon going on living, strengthened by hope.

It is hoped that these notes encourage the reader to look at these poems thoroughly and find out for him- and herself what the poems say, and find an individual significance that may or may not agree with my interpretation.

A BRIEF NOTE ON TRANSLATION FROM ARABIC

To translate from Arabic into any European language is not as easy as translation from one European language to another, where the common roots are mostly Greek or Latin, or both. A synonym is usually not hard to find, even when a minor adjustment is needed. This is not the case in translation from Arabic into English. One thing is that Arabic distinguishes the singular, dual, and plural, which modern European languages do not. The number in Arabic applies to nouns, pronouns, and adjectives. Arabic has masculine and feminine for nouns, pronouns, and adjectives. These qualities cause a great deal of trouble for translation into English in particular; it is perhaps not so difficult to translate into French, for instance, where you have at least a change in the names and adjectives to denote the masculine and feminine. In the rich tradition of Arabic love poetry, the descriptions and qualities are a formidable task for the translator. In describing the beautiful eyes of a woman, we have the dual number to describe two beautiful eyes, and the adjective describing those two eyes. The pronouns referring to the two eyes are also in the dual. This cannot be exactly translated into English because we have to use the one plural form. That made it inevitable for Keats, and other love poets, to speak of "kisses twain" for kissing the two eyes. Then there is extensive reference to poetry and tradition in Arabic that makes it necessary for the translator to explain via footnotes the backgrounds or nuances of particular words. There is also an extreme wealth of adjectives, where no two of those adjectives mean the same thing or carry the same connotations. There is also the multiplicity of nouns for one thing or another. Words like "rain," "cloud," "horse," "lion," "sword," and other names have each dozens, and sometimes hundreds, of different words denoting the same object. This is not easy to translate into English, or probably any other European language. The word "love," for instance, has at least thirty different names, where no two mean the same.

For all these reasons, or some of them, the translation of poetry presents a difficult task for the native speaker of Arabic who is trying to convey the meaning or the tone attached to a certain word, be it a noun, adjective, or verb. But I have done my best in this translation, trying to make it sound as English as possible, sometimes at the expense of losing certain qualities that are too Arabic to be rendered in a non-Arabic language. Therefore, this translation is mainly a translation of the meaning, avoiding the figures of speech or other rhetorical devices that are not the same in one language as they are in another. The medieval Arabic literary dictator Al-Jahiz (775–868) is often quoted as saying that poetry cannot be translated, otherwise its rhythm is lost and its beauty is no longer there. In modern times, the American poet Robert Frost said, "Poetry is that thing which is lost in translation."

If we remain frightened by those two quotations, a great deal of poetry in languages not our own will be out of our reach.

Abdulwahid Lu'lu'a
Cambridge, UK
July 2014

1

Collected Works, Volume 3 (1991)

Shadows of an Israeli Bomber

A notebook,
In it, the children scribbled not a single letter,
A doll with bulging eyes,
In a glimpse of fear,
A ball,
Scattered bread,
And the round mouth of a baby,
Just plucked out of it the murdered mother's nipple,
An arm,
A braid,
Some Hebrew letters,
A time bomb,
Fire brands, smoke, and splinters,
Concrete blocks,
Weeds, soot,
A chair back,

Moans,
Corners,
Two iron bars,
Stretching towards God, like a cross,
A stretch, like something,
And something . . . like wailing.

(pp. 9–10)

I Defend

The Israeli bomber
Returning safe to the base,
Leaving behind a long white trail
(Longer than my arteries,
Longer than the pipelines),
That trail, threatening like the gallows rope,
Is the first line in the song.
But then,
There is no rhythm to fit
The last cries of my children.
Did I say my children?
I have never visited Tyre,
Never stretched on a colored cloth recliner
In a Tyre hotel balcony;
Never sung a first line to the Beirut crowds.
Did I say my children?
I, deprived of the honor
Of being blasted by the love dynamite,
I, the prisoner of war enjoying the right to elect,
I, the citizen, living always
        By the garbage mound,
Did I say my children?
Let the secrets swallow their secrets.
Clarity is complete.
A spiritual peace, unviolated,
Shelling by land and air and sea,
Statements of protest and condemnation,
Children's toys,
Their scattered skulls
Under the tracks of a tank,
        Well green polished,
Evanescing, in the clamor.
The shivering footsteps

Under the remains
Of house utensils,
The tender palms shrunk on rifle steel.
Did I say,
I do not interfere in delicate balances?
I have enough in my frail blood and situation,
Suffice it to me my little question: why?
I will not retain a secret.
The flower is for the apple,
The apple for the stone,
And I bleed alone.
I bleed my hot, honest, talkative blood;
I bleed my mercy-pawned blood
Like a child's neck.
Why? Why?
I realize my private miracle,
And retain no secret.
I did not expect these disappointments.
Yet, gentlemen,
You will not enjoy my weeping.
I will not yield, gentlemen.
You chose my suffering,
And I choose my life and death.
And I know how to defend my only choice,
Gentlemen . . .
Swine . . .

(p. 11)

Samih Al-Qasim

A Report from the Battlefront

From a demolished house
To one where every stone in it
    Shouts to every other stone,
To everything around,
    "Advance"!
From a booby-trapped schoolyard,
The raiders keep on marching
And reach their death
With their debased banner.

Body without a head,
A head without a mouth,
Under a freezing sun,
Shouting in the void.

With my own eyes I saw
A ten-year-old fighter
Walking, but without legs,
With his face towards Nazareth.

With her stunning eyes
And her virgin lips,
With a red rose in her braid,
My sweetheart,
Princess of the seasons,
Resists the heavy cannons.

Out of the camp remains,
They come,

Out of the trenches of defiance,
In a ruined street,
They come,
Out of a cave, of a dilapidated house,
Raising the banner of resistance and defiance,
Spitting their blood on the tank's forehead.
They come with cedar and olives,
With banners,
With fires,
They come.
With the old man's cane,
From the longing of the unborn babe,
They come with love and yearning,
With death and certainty,
They come.
So, stretch out your arms of destruction,
O, you, dragon,
For each of our arms
Is St. George with a sword of fire.

(pp. 17–20)

Was It Necessary?

Was it necessary
For my heart to drop like an unripe apple
From the orphan branch on the family tree
So they can discover the law of love?
Was it necessary
For the pest to spread,
With its manicured nails
    And its glamorous necktie,
    To bury the newborn babies
Before they are given suitable names?
Was it necessary to have
    All this beastly terror,
    Flooding like the moon,
All this lunar silence?
Was it necessary
For us to turn backwards
To all these centuries?

(p. 25)

Coal Buds

News agencies,
In the languages of the entire world,
Announce the death of my completely charred heart,
In the entire languages of the world.
Despite that,
There are new buds
Sticking out their tongues to the flame
And choosing—despite the news agencies—
A straight direction to the sun.
Despite that,
As the newly born
Are more than the dead
(What a wicked consolation!),
Despite that,
The song soars
Over battlefields:
Oh! How beautiful is the red bud,
On the completely charred heart!

(p. 29)

Treachery Hillock

In the low little house
  On the treachery hillock,
There is a table of oak wood
With a lamp on that table
And a book, near that lamp,
  The wind turning over its pages.
The same wind that rattles the windows
At night,
As the moon shows a terribly enchanting face
In the blond night.
The terror of that moon!
The swinging oak branches!
Steps laden with suspicions
Move nearer,
Then move away, terrified,
  And plunge into the void,
Plunge into the void,
Like a stab.

(p. 31)

A Minor Point

In the hall there is space for another corpse.
But the heart is to the brim with nausea.
Anyhow,
You alone can decide.
Oh, beardless young man,
You have space for death.
The multinational death squads
Are awaiting your divine forehead
And your sorrowful eyes,
Oh good-looking youngster,
    Like a volcano,
Enchanting like a hurricane,
How unjustly they were to your burning mouth!
How they delayed the rendezvous of kisses
When they invented your tragic concern
With this minor point:
Life or death.

(p. 35)

The Last Target

In the hospital,
Air bombarded moments ago,
A nurse is helping another nurse;
A dusty tomcat is mewing with terror;
A corpse is protecting another corpse.
There is a flower vase turned over,
Quite undamaged,
Like the bomber returning to base.
The flowers are intact.
The boy, burnt with napalm,
Is licking the brackish vase water,
Spilled with blood,
On the floor of the air bombarded hospital,
Moments ago.
The Red Cross,
The Red Crescent,
The Star of David
(In blue and white, naturally!),
Bounced with the second raid of the bomber
Towards the last target:
That wicked little girl who escaped
The previous raid,
Moments ago . . .

(p. 37)

Anew

On the amputated hand
Is born, anew,
A fact . . . a myth.
In the battered head
Is born, anew,
A sunflower.
In the leg bones
Begins, anew,
The journey of longing.

(p. 39)

Cluster Poem

Aley, or Jizzeen,
Or is it B'aqleen,
Or do you prefer Damoor,
Or is it Beirut,
Oh, Sparrow,
Where will you die?

It grows in rough weather,
My death rose,
The fairest of things,
My firebrand glows under water.

A blue crime
Ploughs through the sea.
A white crime
Creeps across the land.
A crime . . . what color?
Pours from on high.
(If we plant the col . . .)
My blood will circulate the word.

My skull wakes up all night.
The spotted serpent
Stays up all night.
But wail, oh wail-a-way,
The anger of the dead and the living.

A swing in the clouds,
Death in the suburbs,

A little girl, drowned in blood,
Wants her swing
And refuses the ruins.

Who is knocking at the door
At this time?

(p. 43)

What Can Be Done?

They killed him and buried the body by night;
They did not wash the body,
Nor did anyone pray for him
(Even in the other language!)

I had wished to dig up the grave of the murdered,
    To wash the body (I missed my prayer!)
To deliver a funeral oration
    Before some crowd.
But what can be done?
I do not know where the grave is.
And do not know if there is a grave.
I do not know if there is a corpse.
    But I know that the murdered
Climbed by night into God's windows,
And met his end.

I had wished to dig up a grave,
But what can be done?
    Should I dig up my own grave?

(p. 46)

What Wonder!

The dream is you, and you lean on a mountain.
The dream collapses, so does the mountain.
The globe leans on you.
What wonder!
Not a moan of fatigue,
Not a tear of sorrow.
What wonder!
Your heart bursts with overwhelming wrath,
Your death shriek echoes in the entire world,
And the dancing crowd remains,
Busy with the dreaming tune.
What wonder!
The dream carries you to the end of the world,
The dream collapses and your face remains,
A moon unknown is approaching and penetrating me.

(p. 48)

Death Oration

(1)
O, people of the house, come with joy and roses,
And, come along, people of the house.
Cover the newborn baby's body with salt and oil.
(2)
There, he is taking his first step,
Sprinkle his feet with basil water.
(3)
The clever boy went to school;
Come along to scatter sweets to his friends.
(4)
The student succeeded in college,
Sprinkle water on the face of the swooning mother.
(5)
Women are uttering trilling cries of joy,
Let us sprinkle a handful of rice
Over the heads of the married couple.
(6)
The promised fruit is not ripe yet,
Not ripe yet.
There are books he has not read,
Music he has not heard yet,
Works he has not finished,
Babies in the loins of the Arabian prince,
And dreams in tomorrow's loins.
But the tommy gun, tommy gun, tommy gun,
The prophet of the apostate time,
Is delivering its oration,
And the death goblins applaud.

(p. 50)

Asleep

Darkness is coupled with darkness.
A mysterious door squeaks.
Through it shuffles a giant phantom.
The garden leaves shiver.
I saw it stealthily descending
The marble staircase,
Shortening the horizons.
Yet . . . all of you are asleep!

(p. 54)

The 6 p.m. Bus Is Late

On the 6 p.m. bus
Come crowds of rascals from far-off quarters
To the center of night towns,
In search of blue film cinemas,
In search of "a puff"
In a deserted house, in some corner
Ignored by the police . . .
Perhaps, perchance
A lost tourist may cross their way,
A lady holding a handbag
Of money and bracelets.
On the 6 p.m. bus,
I rode from work to death,
And rode from death to work.
I became mean by fatigue
Saddened by my severe anger . . .
For a reason,
Or no reason,
A kid named Ricardos accosted me
—His friends nickname him "Lionheart"—
I was overwhelmed by indescribable rage
And yelled, enough, you son of a bitch,
You impolite!
God damn your father and mother,
And all the riffraff who slipped
  Onto the globe
From the loins of the first billy goat
  In your folks!
The bastard Ricardos drew a knife
From underneath a huge leather belt
And rushed on me.
I did not say my prayers,
But hit the rascal, son of a rascal,

With my rosary.
He stuttered, and staggered,
　　　And reeled, and crumpled
Onto the floor of the bus, dead!
To the site of the accident rushed
The Israeli armed forces
　　　And the U.N. forces.
I cried, "Leave me alone, you folks,
I have enough with my stomach ulcer!"
Dr. Waldheim sighed
And mumbled in a language
　　　I do not understand . . .
Something I could not understand . . .

And the 6 p.m. bus was late!

(p. 76)

Resurrection

Do not grieve, your poor are rich.
Do not despair. . . . Your dead are alive . . .
     A thousand times alive.
Return to your homes,
Let your women propagate.
Ignore your shrouds.
You will come back to life,
In me you will be resurrected.

(p. 55)

The Captive

Do not go out at night, my love.
Do not go out at night.
Your folks are watching you, my love.
And woe! Alas! And woe!
The girls abductor lurks, my love,
Do not go out at night.
The children murderer, also, my love,
And woe! Alas! Be still, my love,
And fear you may be harmed by night,
Do not go out alone, my love,
Do not go out at night.

(p. 62)

Charlie Betton
Does Not Lead the Israelis in the Sinai Desert

When Moses complained to the mount,
God responded from the burning well,
And you
Addressed the wall of the Sinai Desert,
But no one heard your voice, not even the poor,
And no one raised your sword, except the weak,
Charlie Betton,
Do you expect a quick answer,
        From the Lord of the Hosts?
You will not hear except the voice
Of the borne troops, by air, or land, or sea.
You will not hear except the testaments
Of the dead to the dead.
You will not hear, Charlie,
Except the war drums,
Beaten in the dust of the raids.
From Tel Aviv to the Pentagon corridor.
I spoke and you believed.
You spoke and I believed.
Your folks are of my folks,
Charlie!
And Morocco is nearer than Zion!
And I am nearer than
The mythical columns of fire.
Let us go together,
Let us go,
And let us join all longitudes to all latitudes.
And let the banners of refusal
Storm the entire sky around the globe.
Let the hunger cries at the daily banquet
Blow up the granite despotic towers.

(p. 67)

The King's Ring and the Contessa Maria Tereza

And the Italian contessa Maria Tereza,
In the antique market
In one Paris quarter,
She noticed me contemplating
(Across the window shop)
The ring of a deposed king.
She stepped towards me, confidently and calmly,
But I could not see her eyes
(Behind the sunglasses).
She asked, in different languages,
"Who are you?"
I answered, but in Arabic,
"A pauper, and a prince,
A saint and a rogue,
Seduced by a ring of a deposed king."
She said in a royal grandeur,
"I am Contessa Maria Tereza, the Italian."
    I clicked my heels gently,
I turned my cheek away a little,
I bent my head a little
And shouted nobly and warmly,
"I'll be happy if my lady could pay for the ring,
As I have nothing in this world
Except the travel ticket
And my dark resentment."
She paid, and accompanied me to the hotel.

(p. 74)

The Unknown Soldier

He did not return from the war field;
We asked every soldier who returned;
We asked his wounded friends;
We asked the group of prisoners;
We even asked the general.
None of them gave us an answer.
We asked the NC officer;
We asked all who may have had some news of the war.
All that was left for us to ask:
The dead bodies,
The futile and despotic death,
The dunes of sand . . .

(p. 79)

The Rose Plucked Me, My Glass Drank Me

I wore out my woolen vest,
I did not see God's face, nor mine.
Is my faith shaken?
How can I justify death
Of pollen at the orchard gate!
How can I justify my insignificant death,
Deranged in my bed night?
Around me crowded various types of drugs,
My sun setting away from the world,
My conscience falsified all over the world!
I am well prepared,
But what a sorrowful end!
It plucked me,
The rose plucked me.
At the crossroads, I turned right and left,
I could not see anybody.
But the monster was at my heels,
And I could not see her.
No matter.
I thrust my hands in my trousers' pockets,
I chose the longer way, on purpose,
And went on my way.
You know, my sweetheart,
I hide nothing from you.
I felt a little frightened,
And said to myself,
        We'll have some distraction
In this waste.
I started whistling a ready tune,
Which did not save me from my fear,
And behind me was the monster,
After my mortal departure from clear sorrow,
In clear sorrow,

After hunger, weariness, and fatigue,
I threw my head to the monster,
    I cannot hide from you, my sweetheart,
    I could not reach the walls of Al-Quds.
    My glass drank me.
But what a sorrowful end,
My glass drank me!

(p. 83)

Bruxelles, June 6, 1981
(For Bernadette Khidr)

Between waking and nausea
And nausea in drunkenness,
I smell your blood.
Between the storms of forgetfulness
And the firebrand resolve,
I smell your blood.
Secretly,
I smell your blood.
Openly,
I smell your blood.
        In the scent of the cold, dark soil,
In the snow grass and trees,
Shrouded in fading light,
I smell your breath.
And see your betrayed face
On the wind and exile bus window.
In the wasted blood police archives
In the show glass window.
I hear your pulse, haunted by children,
        Flowers, and catastrophe.
In the ticks of a deserted house clock,
In the throbbing of the evening trains.
And I hear your consecrated pulse,
On the beat of oil,
Pumping from my mother's artery
To the industrial towns.
I notice your broken back
In the clamor of airports, stations,
And sudden meetings.
I notice your broken back
Among the gentlemen ambassadors,
Split between fire and water.

You are a bliss . . .
Affection bliss, between relatives and strangers.
A bliss of the poor simpletons.
And you are a scourge,
A scourge on rancor, aggression, and enmity,
A scourge on enemy brothers.
  When you peep out of your grave
To listen to the latest news,
Cain peeps out with his face.
And when the throne of the monkey king
Peeps in the balconies,
And the balcony is of the
  Revolution Command Palace,
And when in free Washington loom
  The bastards of the primitive lies,
Your burning blood screams,
I am Abel,
I am Abel.
Your pain builds up with fire,
And the heart withers,
Withers the jellylike blood rose,
Withers Bernadette's face,
And withers the jasmine and jelly flower
Over foggy Europe's bricks.
With the palm trees and the wedges,
In the hellish Bedouin wastes.
I'll preach with your prophetic name
From East to West
And call the seed of love for a witness,
And call for a witness,
The essence of things and man.
How you were born
In the shades of your lemon,
And how you were killed in man,
And how you took revenge for man;

When you were resurrected
In the moons of your olive,
I'll preach with your prophetic name
From East to West,
And call for witness the children's surprise,
How the smoke of your pipe
Froze in the wide expanse
To draw a blind little girl,
And the black death tulip
Against a red background.
      How the smoke of your pipe
      Froze in the wide world space
To draw with that sweet blood
Tomorrow's elevations
Looted from your Palestine eyes.
I smell your blood
And see in the distance your banner,
Fluttering on some mythical spaces
And raising from sleep of death
      The spirit of jasmine and jelly flower,
Sewing the wheat of birth
In the land of waste conscience,
In the land of waste conscience,
In the land of waste conscience.

Namur, Belgium, August 31, 1982
(p. 100)

Children . . . and My Children

Children are born,
Received on the birth beds
    By their chosen names
From the revered forefathers tree.
Received by saving programs,
A long look to the future,
Received by the scent of boiled cinnamon,
On the fire of longing,
Received by birthday parties
And other feasts,
And new clothes.

My children are born,
Received by tears of love
And the shiver of fear.
At the gates of maternity hospital,
    Waiting for them
Are the mad dogs' eyes.
Waiting for them
Are the police clubs.
Waiting for them
Are the body liquidation programs
And the long look to death.
My children are born;
With them are born
Their white phosphorus bombs
With their marvelous lights
Like the fireworks
Of the carnival.
My children are born
    With their little coffins.

(p. 111)

Resurrection

Curtains flutter in the wind.
The night shivers
In the catastrophic shriek.
In semi-sleep,
In semi-death,
By the light of a refrigerator,
Semi-open,
The hungry cat passes by.
I pull the quilt on my frozen nose,
And in my silent fear,
The starched cloth rubs
Against my eyelashes flicker.
In semi-sleep, in semi-death,
By the light of a silent bomb,
The killed man gets up
And walks . . .

(p. 115)

War Victims

A sparrow, with a severed wing,
Was tired of the winds
And fell in some battlefield

~~~

O, cannons!
Wheat stalk and a rose,
On the limits of the forest,
Where is the return road?
O, tank!
A white cloud,
A bomber,
Cutting like a knife
In the sky tent.

~~~

Who taught the snipers
To pierce the book?
Who taught the snipers
To pierce the lovers' letters
And the lovers' photos?
Who taught the snipers,
O, bullet?

(p. 117)

Revenge of the Dead

Should I wake my tired wife?
My children, dead on the lawn, will startle.
No!
It is an embarrassing situation.
They come without appointment.
They entered the house, without invitation.
Dead after dead they arrive.
They turn on all the lights,
In a clatter.
They fling their shrouds in the corners,
Wander among seats,
Around the beds,
Blue, naked,
      Going past the mirrors.

I shriek indignantly,
Enough!
You are crossing my limits,
Enough!
You are breaking promises,
Enough!
You, dead,
Leave me alone,
Leave me to my sorrow,
Leave me to my silence,
My shame, my death.
Can't you see the cup is empty?
Companions, leave me,
      I gulped, to the lees, the cup of madness,
Leave me . . .

(p. 119)

Rendezvous

A forehead and nine fragments,
And two cave eyes.
Who could see me but myself?
Good-bye, my sweetheart,
Good-bye. I shall see you one day,
I shall see you among the mirror fragments.

(p. 125)

Punishment Song

The criminals, all, I knew,
I knew the criminals, all.
I knew them one by one,
From every point,
In every tongue.
And I shall chase them throughout life,
And I shall punish them after death,
And they will not escape.
I said, shall not escape.
They are right here
Between my hand and heart.

(p. 79)

The General's Possessions

On the general's table, there stands a vase;
In the vase stand five roses.
On the general's tank spring five muzzles . . .
Under the general's tank lies a five-year-old child,
And a rose.
On the general's shoulder lie five stars and child;
In his vase sink five children and a rose.
Under his tank
Lie five roses and five children.
The tank has innumerable muzzles . . .

(p. 131)

A Meeting in Exile

Along the far sunset: my heart and eye
>Stand between me and what departure hides . . .
Along the far sunset: two cups of wine,
>A gasp that flutters in between two hands.
I said, hello, I have waited too long,
>You said, hello, two exiles! What surprise!
We laughed in agony, and then we cried,
>In that evening that fell on two expired . . .

(p. 252)

Europeans

They go out, evenings, for their garden stroll;
The gentle, pampered dogs
Around them leap.
The minor ones, who are so clean,
Cling to a dreaming shop window.
They go out in the evening,
Answer the greeting with a bow,
Annoyed (with arrogant reserve)
With the primitive din
Of a foreign family.
They go out, evenings,
     For their garden stroll.

(p. 258)

Severance

They come into the morning
With conflagration rites.
I did not find her in the heap of flesh.
They said,
"They saw her at the start of shelling.
She was behind the last sandbag."
And said,
"They saw her in a ditch, afar,
Splintering, with a baby face in her arms."
She was fighting, it was said.
I did not find her.
I ran to search for her, throughout the night,
From one alley to another.
I asked the folks about her;
They said, "A cooing we have heard
And saw lilies and ears of corn."
I did not find her,
Then I called.
My voice echoed in the corners of the camp.
A shell embraced me in horror,
Then scattered me on ruined homes.
At dawn she came to see me.
She did not find me there.
But in her hands there was
A dead child's face
With some grenades . . .

(p. 260)

A Mine

He left the house at dawn, as usual,
To go to work,
But in the police post his wife whooped,
"I made his tea,
He moved the green basil
Off his black hair.
He greeted me, pulled back the covers
Over the children of happy nights.
He wooed me for a while,
And disappeared in his red scarf,
Stretching to the door."
"I am going to work."
His wife, in terror whooped.
The neighbors wondered,
"He briskly greeted us, was clear,
No light, no shadow.
He got on the bus at dawn:
"I am going to work". . . .
A man, of the valley lilies
And the mountain sumac trunks.
He went . . . but did not reach . . .
Returned . . . but did not reach . . .
A certain man
Left home at dawn . . .

(p. 265)

A Waltz for the Air Raid

Turn on the light.
Open the other window.
The roar of planes
Is coming
From some horizon, lost among directions.
They are about to shell us,
So let us dance now
To the soft Mozart tunes.
One minute only we still have
In this life.
Oh, you whom I adore.
In this moment of life,
Rise to the waltz,
Give me a tender hand,
In the elegant moment of death.
Turn on the light.
The roaring planes
Are showering stars now
And lighting memories.

(p. 314)

How?

Addressing the platforms of dead cities,
I ask them how can they not be angry?
I stop the caravan of creeping savages
To ask how can they not feel so ashamed
For executing a pregnant lady
To kill her unborn baby?

(p. 135)

Shylock

With an Yves Saint Laurent tie,
And a Pierre Cardin suit,
And a pipe.
In a head kerchief and band,
In a chapeau,
In a sombrero . . . or cylindrical headgear
He tours the capitals, free at large,
And weeps with his victims tears.
He weeps, disappears, and then appears.
He laughs over the profit
In the death stock exchange,
Shylock!
Speaks in every tongue,
Sure of every direction,
He besieges me . . . my hand is too weak.
My silence is detained,
     My voice is too detained.
He seeks my death.
I ask,
"In which bank do you invest my death,
Shylock?"
But Shylock
Asks me the same question!

                    (p. 398)

Taxi Driver

Outside the town limits, they stopped you.
You did not hesitate.
You dreamt of a generous fare
For the easy trip.
You said in your naïve conscience
    (Now they are caught!
    The stupid foreigners
    Are not aware of our official fares)
They are going to a settlement

You spoke to them of your chronic pains.

When they discharged their pistol magazine,
In your naïve temple
An almond tree (perhaps) shivered
And a minaret wept.

                                             (p. 520)

Butterfly

By chance,
You hovered round the red rose,
By chance.

⸻

The black helicopter hovered,
By chance.

⸻

It fired the color bomb
At the pupils,
By chance.

⸻

It fired the gas bomb
At the house,
The almond tree,
And the rose,
By chance.

⸻

You were in the rose,
In the color, in the gas,
And by chance,
Death closed a balcony against the scene.

(p. 528)

Last Letter

Two hands on the rubble,
A face peeping from the dream,
Remains of a stupid innocent cat,
A boy passing by the shells' memory,
Bleeding, bleeding,
Cold, frightened,
A mother mewing,
To a bomber, with angel wings. . . .
At the moment of shelling we were there,
Three prisoners,
Nine dead,
And seven wounded.
At the moment of sniping,
We were there,
        Three wounded,
Nine prisoners,
And seven, dead.
At the moment of dreaming,
        We were there,
Three dead,
Nine dead,
And seven, dead.
And a bomber with angel wings . . .

(p. 133)

Mosaic on the Dome of the Rock

What is your name, Bride?
Did you forget me?
 "Yebus!"

A night over the alcoves,
A minaret dazed in time,
A woman at the door,
Suspicions of a passing tourist,
And foreign soldiers.

A hillock for death and life,
Shall I call you,
Or a turban for God?

The barefoot boy,
Asking history for shoes,
Filling the markets with his call:
"I sell the healing balm,
For impotence, baldness, and the black spot."

I am here,
So breathe
My holy rock.

Oh, wall, oh, towers,
Never mind our intimate secrets,
Many a conqueror tried to shake the lock
To violate our ancient soul

But returned defeated.
I see in you the beginning.
My tomorrow will be yesterday.

Don't deprive me the blessing of the prayer,
Oh, the duty of ablution.
No water for the sore feet.
No water of holiness.

My blood is on the rababa.
Who will chant for the Prophet
        And his Companions?

My heart is with you,
Oh! Then, oh!
And your dead heart
Is under the invaders' feet.

The sarcophagus jewel
Shines at night.
Pray for us,
Pray,
Oh, Goddess of rites.

The golden ring
Is on the Arab finger.
Who has severed the finger?
Praise Him who endowed;
Wail to him who lost.

The white barefoot little girl
Runs on the water . . .

The eyes differ,
The look in the eyes differ,
Oh! Mount Olive!

Oh! Arcades,
Do not draw the drapes.
I came back from abroad,
I came back from collapsed memory,
With all the rites the soul can hold.

Hush, hush!
This is the horses' neighing,
Shaking the heart of night.

Ghifar, oh, Ghifar,
Do not block the way.
I am only a friend,
Reviving the waste.

You scolded;
It did not work.
Oh, my master 'Umar!

The Muslim cavalier is resting
By an olive tree.
Jesus the lord
        Peeps out of an icon.

I saw Juha's nail,[1]
Its loss exists.
I saw Juha's nail,
Its existence is lost.
I saw Juha's nail
In the Jewish quarter.

Do not begin the greeting.
Listen . . . don't you hear
The breathing of the walls?
Listen a bit, young man,
Then begin the greeting.
Afterwards take to your heels
The way you like.

Oh, for you, oh!
Read and do not read.
This is God's book.
The sun is in the shelter.

The Qurmoti in me,
Oh, poor people of the Earth,
Pray on the prophet,
This is the time of refusal.

1. Juha sold a house, provided he kept possession of the nail left on the wall.

Ladders of yearning
Ascend across clouds.
Oh, Buraq cavalier,[2]
Our steeds are saddled with oppression.

I came from Kufah[3]
To write the verse.
  The sun is eclipsed.
Who will take me to the quest?

Pray over the murdered,
Comfort his relatives,
I came to bail him out,
From his heavy death.
My armies are olives and palm trees.

I am a descendant of the god Lat,
My father is the god Ba'al
I was baptized in the Nile, the Jordan, the Euphrates.
I am a descendant of the god Lat,
I walk—behind me is the sun—
To the fields of Al-Quds.
I walk . . . my shadow is the night.

(p. 209)

2. Al-Buraq, the steed the Prophet rode in his ascent to heaven.
3. Kufah, a town southwest of Baghdad, home of several revolutionary leaders.

The Intifadah
(Uprising)

(A Letter to Invaders Who Do Not Read)
Advance, advance!
The sky above you all is Hell,
The land beneath you all is Hell,
Advance!
Our child and aged die
But will not surrender.
The mother falls
On her murdered child
But will not surrender.
Advance!
With your troop carriers,
With your malice launchers,
And threaten,
And displace,
     And make orphans,
And pull down,
You won't disrupt our depths,
You won't defeat our desires,
We are decisive fate.
Advance!
Behind you is your way,
Behind you is your future,
Behind you is your sea,
Behind you is your land.
But still there is before us
Our way and our future,
Our land and sea.
Our good and evil.
What is it that sends you
From a corpse to a corpse?
And how can it lead you,

From idiocy to idiocy,
That book of madness?
Advance.
Behind this stone there is a palm.
Behind the grass there is your end.
After the corpse there is a trap,
So fair and well-designed.
If one leg could be saved,
Remain a forearm and a wrist.
Advance!
Hell is every sky above you.
Hell is every land below you.
Advance!
Your taboo is with us allowed,
And your allowed is here taboo.
Advance!
With your desire to kill,
Which is going to kill you.
And aim with merciless decision,
And level at the womb;
There is a drop of our blood,
And it is raging now.
Advance!
Whichever way you like
And kill.
Your killer is acquitted,
Our murdered is accused.
The Lord of Hosts is still awake, and up;
So is the criminal judges' judge.
Advance!
Do not open a school,
And do not close a prison,
Do not apologize,
And do not be wary,
And do not understand.

Your first is your last,
Your faithful is your unbeliever,
Your malady is chronic.
So do not restrain, and so indulge,
And push forward,
And rise and clash,
To the final stage that is left for you,
To the final rope that is left for you,
For every stage must have an end,
And every rope must have an end.
Do not listen nor understand.
        Advance!
Hell is every sky above you,
Hell is every land below you,
Not the soldier's helmet.
Not the policeman's club.
Not your tear gas.
Gaza is crying for us
Because it is a part of us,
As the ferocity of the absent
In his bleeding yearning to return.
Advance!
From street to street,
From house to house,
From corpse to corpse.
Advance!
Every violated stone
        Cries in anger
As does cry every field.
And every nerve is roaring:
Death, but not kneeling.
Death, and no kneeling.
Advance!
Here is the camp advancing,
Here is the wounded and this slaughtered,

And the bereaved, and the orphaned.
Houses' stones advanced,
And the youthful wheat stalks,
The suckling, aged, and the widows,
Doors of Nablus and Jenin,
They have also advanced,
With windows of Jerusalem,
The sun prayer,
With incense and with condiments,
They all advanced to fight,
Advanced to fight.
Do not listen, and do not understand,
And advance!
Hell is every sky above you,
Hell is every land below you. Advance!

(pp. 405–11)

Asking No Permission

I ask nobody's permission.
Quietly, carefully,
I pluck my sorrow damask rose,
And sing,
To my captive body sweetheart.
I ask nobody's permission.
Quietly, carefully,
I hurl my stone
At the face of the globe
And sing
To the storms of wrath
In the night of humanity.
I ask nobody's permission.
I bite my death apple
And sing, and sing
To freedom.

(p. 322)

The King

The hurricane king
Is coming, but coming without sails,
Bathing in time's water,
Dreaming of the bride,
Promising the rites.
He is coming, but without carnival.
The hurricane king
Is coming.
Ah! Shall the masques drop down?

(p. 331)

Departure Song

The balcony basil withered.
My love, come back a little.
There are gold finches in my mouth for you,
And orchards in my chest,
And deer in my lap,
My love.
Come back young, strong, and handsome.
There are poems in my eyes for you,
    And moons,
And dawns, in my hands.
And noble babes,
My love, and wheat stalks in my hair for you,
And around my waist grow almonds and pears,
And round my legs are steeds and anklets,
A plain, and brooks.
My love, come back a little,
Come back for more.
For you I have prepared flowers and wine,
For you I have prepared the bed,
On the dead pavement,
A land and sky,
Children and homes,
My love, come back for more, for less.
The balcony basil withered.

(p. 40)

Thunderbolt

Two arms of stone
Slowly emerge from the grave.
A lark ruffling in a pool of blood,
An army truck.
I sing for you now,
    Oh, bullet,
Waking the heart from its illusion.
Oh, baby shriek in the womb.
I sing for you now, approaching in a shell.
Two arms of narcissus,
Slowly emerging from the mire.
A song that cannot be sung
A thunderbolt in a vase.

(p. 339)

The Invaders

They came out of their stone graves,
Bent with their sorrows,
Silent on their rage,
Obscure.
They came out,
Lime dust dropping off their bones,
On the feeble steps
Seep the smells of death and jasmine.
In the rubble of the graveyard,
They found a child without parents.
They ate him, and they prayed
     On two corpses.
They came out of their stone graves.
They tumbled in their nightmares.

(p. 341)

Yearning

I no longer have a hope in my beard.
It fell under the blade of the wind,
One hair after another.
It fell at the morning gate.
I no longer have a hope
In my homeland exile.
Here I am coming back
    From my hand;
Coming back,
Not to me;
Coming back in the pollen.
A palm tree in the gulf
Yearns for my palm tree,
And I am coming back
From the ripeness of dates.
So listen to my call,
    And witness my step,
Oh, Arabian lands!

                  (p. 346)

The Phoenix

The swallow burned.
It burned thus:
In the ashes all balances are equal.
Fire and wind,
Fire and water,
Water and wind.
Oh, you who are coming from wood, burn
In Christ's cross.
The swallow burned.
The meager ashes are a little rise
Between the cradle of the newborn
And the graves of the murdered.
I said that this wing is this spring,
Oh, people, I said, listen to my corpse,
I said.
But no one listens.
  My call
Is lost in the desert.
And the swallow burned.
Oh, she burned,
A heap of ashes
Too fast asleep.
  Ah, and was scattered,
Ah, and disappeared.
The phoenix fire is a sarcastic song,
I said. It did not rise.
The swallow burned
And here begins the other life.

(p. 352)

~ 2 ~

Elusive Land (1995)

Death Certificate of the Last Dinosaur

He surprises their feasts and dies, the last dinosaur. His birth certificate was scattered by storms at night, before the end of its last section, with the last dream. . . .

(I, the rebel, witnessed the death and I declare)

There is nothing but darkness: a wing fluttering over the deep, a wind hissing; nothing but giant trunks of acacia, bared by meteors. There is nothing but the moaning of the rocks on the cliff. It is a heavy night. Huge skeletons and ashes are on the surface of the water in the stagnant pool. . . .

There are snow clouds passing over the forehead of the aggrieved dinosaur and his sluggish look. . . .

A shiver hits me. . . . Now it inhabits me, now I inhabit him . . . the only dinosaur and his extinct progeny. There is nothing but the drop of temperature below the limits of nature. Nothing but the distant stars dimming in the darkness of the incoming tear. . . .

He surprises their feasts and dies. The croaking of the frogs is his elegy in the silent night. He resents the throes of death. There is no time for throes. He has no taste for grandeur in death. His mother said to him one day: provide for your death with dignity, and do not care for rites.

His mother said to him: die as the suns desire to die. (I, the rebel, witnessed the death and I declare): the time was hard. And in the forehead of the suffering dinosaur was on the move a vein with oozing tears and tongues of flame.

And anger moaned on both his lips.

Here the volcanoes retrieve a memory they have lost of late. Here explode the roses of dejection as fire and light. The question fluctuating in the space of the soul bursts: Oh, initiator of the beginning, how could the end be a blind secret? And how can times begin after staying so long on a reclining earth, after the collapse of the ice mountains?

With two foggy eyes, he tours the besieged space (sea and sand), surveying the horizon of ends (sand and sea). Surprised by a flicker in the ashes, he sheds roses on what the earth bears of graves.

I whisper a massacre lullaby.

(I, the rebel, heard this secret weeping. And I say):

Here is the spring, jetting from a crevice in its rock, an herb imploring two sparrows from the clouds. A gentle breeze is gargling in the reeds of the plain. A little shepherd and a flock of butterflies are courting a black thorn, swaying coquettishly. A damsel is peeping out of a high balcony, on a boy not from this neighborhood. She lowers to him a golden hair to ascend. A flute is moaning in the shade of a bending olive tree. A bomber in the air is vomiting its intestines on the earth, and scatters its bloody shrieks.

(I heard the weeping and I say):
A new year, roaming with laughter, is drunk, in the battlefield.
A lady in maternity bed is sobbing in shame.
The virility of her enemies, coming with an enemy god, reminds of the
    besieged embryo.
"Oh, Lord, take it and take me," wailing before falling on the bench with
    her terrible pains.
Blood is wondering about its secret.
Bodies lie in the fields.
A land is with no hope.
Who would steady from the stumbles?
Who would straighten from the falls?
And retrieve the old splendor?
A blood wonders.

A chant trembles among the temple marbles.
"Oh, Lord, take us and take them" . . .
And Lord, leave us and leave them.
And oh, Lord, be a judge between us.
They judge the wheat with death by hunger.
The lure the songs to their death.
They inscribe their doctrines on our door arches.

They write in our letters a language resented by languages. And Lord, you command us and we obey. You guide us and we get lost. Oh, Lord, we are among the ruins of prophecies, creep to our desires. We stopped for long, we walked for long. On thorns and firebrands, our feet left their flesh. And on we went. And on the wind we put our names and the headstones of our dead. Nations beat us on our sorrow. Bitter weeping did not lead us to an oasis. Heat has burned our bodies.
Where should we go?
No roads can lead to any horizon or land.

In the trap fell the aged martyrs. Their power failed them. Before penetrating through the wretched earth, they cried, "Peace". . . . They cried, "Peace," and were gone. . . . Neither who nor what! The shell dust fell as final silence. . . . And here is the final dinosaur bidding farewell to his beloved dead, yearning to his departed folks, alone. Alone, alone, besieged by lightning and thunder, his limbs are in the ice, his eyes two holes in the stuttering of distant ozone. The factory smoke is his trees, no fruit, and no water. Here he is writhing in his shadow. Fragmenting on the turning earth, naked and shamed, shouting "Peace" but none. . . .

He turns into gel. His sorrow was surprised by the sovereign power. He looks over his death and dies.

This space narrows, the wind widens. The Lote Tree spreads its branches. Oh, people, where have you disappeared? How did you end? Then rose a shy question from the last dinosaur just leaving: "After me will be civilization?" Okay. Let the nations of light come at their pace. Here I am folding my darkness and wedding kerchief and quitting from the nations' memories.

Let civilization come as a new dawn without me. I am tired, exhausted; the spirit powers in my extensive body have withered. Let me shrink then, as the laws of nature would have me. Here I evanesce, slowly, slowly. Here I am erased from my last shadow on the earth. This is my refuge. This is my resort, and here I disappear.

And bury my soul on the darkening star.
The last dinosaur has passed out of life.
The security staff can rest for a while, can rest for long.
They can manicure their nails and brush their teeth.
The police stations can sip their tea in peace.
The pretty women can attract handsome men.
    The good statesmen may take their parties two hours to the dawn.
    The laborers may have their work, the farmers their hope.
    And the travelers can have their kisses.
For the arrival, long life!
And here is the last dinosaur
    Surprising his sorrows
    In the sovereign power.
He looks at his death and dies.

(pp. 7–16)

Midnight Physiognomy
In the Dream-Deprived Mariners' Café

I shall not pass again by this obstinate hell.
I shall not revisit the madness horizon.
A wave hurled out my corpse
From the high seas to a narrow shore
In the quiet country.
Halt the sea!
I cannot bear the ends outside their time.
I cannot bear the travel behind unstable directions,
And the fall of victims on memories' altar,
And expecting what shall not be.
And I see them now,
And I know them now,
My brothers, the dream-deprived.
Midnight is their coffin.
Their pipes bend with fatigue
From a distance unseen,
On a horizon, unseen.
They spit out their sorrows
    In the smoke of yearning.
One of them
Has his wig
    Turning grey by long exile
From his loved ones and home.
One other,
His daughter hanged herself by her braid
(When she became pregnant, her friend ran away).
One of the others,
His good wife deserted him
And disappeared, with his terrible passions.
Another still,
His buttock was bitten by a shark
And lice invaded his beard.

His admiring lovers deserted him to other mariners.
Still one other
Mastered despair and the cup,
Bleeding and playing music
In the bar of the old dead folks.
One other
Was an invalid in his chair,
Staring forever
At the fragments of the foam.
And one
Will be killed in a sorrowful accident
The day after tomorrow.
Still, one
Was not borne by anyone. . . .
I shall not pass again by this obstinate hell.
My tropical blood plant cannot bear the snow.
My hat was snatched by the storms
(With my head inside it).
The flow of the sea wave returned
(With my arm on it).
The roads took the passers' steps
(With my leg on them).
What is left of my body
Is not enough to feed
The hungry folks of the town.
I am following the straight path of my blood,
Going,
And shall not pass by this hell.

(pp. 23–27)

A Letter from Tawfiq Zayyad

The dear earth is very dear to me,
     And a little heavy on my forehead,
     Mouth, and hand.
And I, as you know,
I do not like thick darkness,
The long monotonous boring silence;
But I manage the wicked yearning
From my stay, far away,
From my homeland and flowers,
     My homeland people,
My homeland sun,
Its unbelievable flock of sparrows.
I manage the separation of road
From my blood road
And the stubborn songs' atmosphere.

My dear friends,
I am still at the start of the coming trip,
After my last death, at the entrance
     Of the sinful paradise!
My friends,
I am still busy with the tiresome dialogue
With the despotic gang
And their brutal history nightmares.

Eh! Never mind.
I wonder how you are now, my friends!
Are you still very busy whispering
     To dim images?
Well, my trip is still the same:
On my way I met people called
"People of the Insurgents Convent."

They live in the mountain caves, naked,
Their food is oak fruit,
In the cloud beds they have virgin women.
Their coffins are full of pure gold
		And rare jewels.
They reside in the mountain caves,
Without memories or songs.
Their silence is their water.
Their passions have the fire rhythm
		Among caves,
And the remains dust.
I visited them after my recent death.
I fenced with them in distant songs and rays.
Then I befriended them in the rites of loss.
They are good. They gave me a warm welcome.
They showed me their sleeping sites in the ashes.
In the halls I met some skeletons,
Which frightened me a little.
They hurried to me gently
And whispered intimately,
		"Some of our ancient forefathers." . . .
Then bowed a figure, standing to attention,
		At their door.
(He is the old pagan guard,
And their priest, from thousands
		And thousands of years).
I visited them after my death,
One evening, soaked by freezing rain.
They built the fire for me
		In their forefathers' altars.
Their princess warmed me
		In a bed of water and bamboo
With a quilt of rose, jasmine,
		Palm, and daisies.
I said, "You are then from olden times,

The people of the Insurgent Convent?"
They laughed and cried,
    And returned my dry clothes,
And returned life to me.
I said, "What is your tomorrow?"
They lit their beacons
In every direction,
And disappeared in the mountain caves,
Beyond the land of questions.

The night journey went long,
    Then I met some of their grandchildren,
    In the fog.
I greeted them . . . but they turned away.
I noticed some scars on the faces
    Of pregnant ladies.
I asked, "What happened
    To my old companions?"
A rebel, passing by, said to me,
"The secret of the Insurgent Convent
    Is profound."
I continued my song in the obstinate road:
What happened to my old companions?
And to my orphan children?
And to Um-al-Amin, who was exhausted
By my sorrowful explosions
And my fits of wrath,
At a world exhausted, by its beacons.
So it retrieved the darkness
Able to see but assuming blindness.

My friends, staying in the land
    Of tears and blood,

My friends, remember my message
And spread my banner.
Night travel may take long
    In the waste of years,
And the wilderness may be short.
Oh, brothers and companions,
Perhaps the atmosphere that you witness
Is not what you witness
Of an atmosphere in the labyrinths
    Of your sorrow
And the hidden corners of madness land . . .
I did not mean . . .
    But my departure is imminent
From the heights of Galilee
To ride in the formidable time machine.
Brothers and companions,
    Remember my call
And guard my rose
Against the seasons' winds and fires.
Dear friends, brothers, and companions
Yes, my world is my world.
I said that yesterday.
And there is no silence
    In my language today.
No silence in my banner,
And will say tomorrow what I say:
Perhaps we shall meet
In our next season's celebrations.
My world is still my world.

Space was not impatient with my steps.
Vigor was not impatient with my blood.
My lung was not impatient with the winds.
My body was not impatient with the wounds.

I was not impatient with the nights
    Ruminating their days.
I was not impatient with my yearning
    To my dream's sun
And the slowness of the morn.
I said, this way
Will lead tomorrow . . . or tomorrow . . .
    To the noble aim,
In the heights of Galilee.

I was alive equal to my love of life.
So remember me
    As much as memories desire.
And remember me
When the cup rings against the cup,
Proud of the tune of the cord,
When a nation rebels
Against its sorrow and triumphs,
When a graceful figure sways
    In the moonlight,
When a rebellion brightens,
When a little girl laughs,
When an almond tree flowers,
When a rose opens,
When the sweetheart meets the mate,
When the emigrant returns
    After an exhausting exile.
Remember me in your birthdays,
In your children's weddings,
Let my step be in your steps,
To the laborers' paradise,
And the sun of human beings.
Remember me when death branches
    Grow green

And bathe in the dewy fragrance.
A forest in the distance,
In the land of love, and beauty, and fruit.
I was alive equal to my love of life.
So, remember me,
As much as memories desire.

True . . . no joy among us was complete.
True . . . no call calmed down.
True . . . we were raided
By security and sorrow,
By the Army and levity,
In every feast.
And the police used us for diversion,
And the Army too.
True . . . they never gave a chance
     For a song to start.
True . . .
But we never lowered our foreheads
     Or succumbed to fetters,
With feet fixed in steps
     Or forearms tight.
True, suffering increased,
But we did not shiver
     In fear of increase.
Oh, my companions,
We loved life as life wished,
So remember me as memories wish.
Remember me and collect the dispersed,
And give a chance to the singer's sorrow
To come back a little,
To the joy of singing.

To conclude . . .
But there is no conclusion;
Remember me to my family,
To my brothers,
To my residential quarter,
Remember me to my revolution,
To my banner,
And farewell.

(pp. 41–54)

The Road

I have faith in the desert.
All those who ran to the sea
Have legs of reed.
They are not of the water people,
When we count them,
Nor of the fire people.
I have faith in the desert.
Let the dead stumble on the dead,
And let the living follow
In the light of my steps in the long night,
Until the shining of the blood,
In the height of the day.

(p. 64)

Palestine First

A female martyr's meal is enough
For two male martyrs.
        Oh, mother wind . . . Oh, tired Hagar,
Prepare the little food for your children,
Returning on the exile carts.
Use my shroud as a tablecloth
For the old dishes.
Go and spread my kafiyyeh head kerchief
For the dear guests.
They are tired and hungry.
Prepare a meal for them
From the waste herbs.
Prepare the cups of suffering
And the jar of your terrible sorrows.
Bread and salt will soon bring us together,
And our torn-off limbs will be gathered
By the good morsel of return,
And the banquet on the bench.

A female martyr's meal is enough
For two male martyrs.
No, our trained systematic death was not in vain,
No, we were not lost,
Not drunk with our dreams.
The traps have known us well for ages.
And here we confess:
We have scattered flowers
On the guillotines, for ages.
The professional killer enjoyed playing with our necks.
The conquerors passed through our bodies
As they desired, all that they desired.

We offered the crocodiles of blood river
    Our charming damsels.
We spread our call banner in the sleep of darkness,
We vowed our rifles to all directions,
We dug our trenches
In the language of the sands.
Never mind!
The adulterer dictated the terms of chastity to us
The masters of adultery taught us
    Dancing in the martyrs' obsequies.
The despot's lash lectured us on people's freedom.
Never mind!
We are traitors of our dead,
Rising today from our death.
Shaking off today and now, from our flesh,
The dust of repeated speech,
And a silence overdue,
And a wound that congealed.
And here we are, children of our own quarters,
Returning on the exile carts
From the humming of the massacres,
And the gurgles of the axles,
The mumbling of graveyards,
And the cries in prisons.
Yes, coming back,
On the winds' horses,
In the carts of madness.

Peace, then, is this war?
Rose, then, is the jet of blood?
Wheat, the widows' tears?
Did God burden man more than he could bear?
God knows what you know but you don't . . .

I have the clamor of beings.
In the beings is peace. In them is tranquility.
Peace, then, was the war?
War, then, was the baby yearning for his mother?
Then come what come may!
Come what come may!

A swallow from the shelling fragments,
A willow from the bereaved cries and flames of fire,
Invite their sparrows to the final calls in the nest.
The shadow of smoke in God's words on earth
Are written by God for the believers:
That the plenty is little,
The little is plenty in the eyes of niggardly time.
The wind does not declare its secrets,
The soil does not divulge what the sun said to the roots.
Nor is the mother asked about her blood
That flowed into the embryo's veins.
I do not ask the rocks about Canaan's heart,
My ancient grandfather,
Nor do I claim Phoenicia's crown, my niece,
Suffice was it to me my Hijazi glory.
I joined Najd to Najd to the apex of creation,
I traveled on every possible horizon,
Then I returned and joined my shade,
And the shades of prophethood,
At the Lote Tree.
The butterflies befriended me,
The beasts of the wild enjoyed my company.
In every land I have been,
And where I ended I began.
Residing in this earth . . . it willed and I willed.
But it deluded me mercilessly,

So I burned in its chest and was put out;
Then I re-burned and was put out again.

⟿

Elusive is this earth!
Her pivot is the eye pupil. Her game is to see me,
And not see me.
Elusive . . . a bitch . . .
Her hobby is to slaughter her lovers
With lily blades.
I lured her, but she turned away.
She lured, and I braided her hair passionately,
With my blood silk and song roses.
She repented and ignored me,
As if, in her eyes, I was not even an atom
In place, or a moment in time.
        Elusive is this earth,
A slayer, but, in the end, she is my child.
My kingdom in her living heart,
Of her rock is my scepter,
Of her grass is my pallium . . .
Elusive, she exhausted me,
As a king or a slave, hurting to her name.
Unjust is this earth in her justice,
And just in her injustice.
Death disported with me;
It besieged me for a little dream in her dream,
And death gave me the choice:
If it should buy me or I buy it.
I baptized it, and made peace with its bad manners,
And all its deferred dates,
Because my life, in God's law, became its wife
And I am one of its children.
Death disported with me for long.
How it despises me, and how I despise it,

With no regret or excuse.
And how it despises,
    An old pigeon, that can coo well on my roof!

Pigeons settling on my roof,
New clouds on the morning balconies,
Peace on the lifetime wrath,
Day by day, month by month, year by year,
Peace on my ulcer and my nights of waiting.
Peace on my disaster, my setback, my defeat.
Peace on my joy for my triumph,
And the footfall of steps returning home,
In the stuttering of the road,
And the tyranny of the walk,
And the remote destinations.
Peace on me as I shake hands with my grief
And build my fire at the top of death.

The rebec moans, yearning to its poet's hand.
Oh, my rebec homeland,
May your call be answered.
Stretch out your hands
With henna of the martyr wound,
And with the homeless tears.
Pray for the hostage grief.
Pray with the victim's glory.
And moan, and groan, and while, and sing,
On my forearm, oh my rebec homeland.
And stretch your hands,
Your prophet is coming to you
With his verses
And his banners
And with his regiments of companions.

Here opens the grief its golden window
For the worshippers of day's sunlight.
Here is the innocent balcony basil,
The tears mint,
And the child, stripping the bandage off his wound
And flying to the schoolyard.
Here are the workers returning
With bags of fruit and bread
From a construction site,
From the workshop of water, rose, and electricity,
From the roads of new struggle and its sunny yards,
From the steel plant, from the tourism installations,
From the nursery of almonds and elder,
From the quarry of rocks and dignity.

And here the seasons reclaim the seasons,
The mountains relate their legends,
    And the plains repeat.
Here we shall collect our features,
Restore our names,
And shall count the victims
In the flesh of our souls,
    And the marble of our graveyards.
We shall set in the martyrs' names,
    Draw a map of heroic sufferance,
Call in our children on the feast night
From the ends of the earth.
We recall our children,
Adopt the orphans of our beloved.
We resume the old weeping,
    And ask God's forgiveness,
And shall build our museums in the ditches

Of our remains, and pray separately and jointly.
We shall weep and laugh,
  Weep and laugh the way we like.
We shall dance in every square,
Wink at our beauties, and fly on the rhythm of our dabkas
In a space that chases the invaders' gas
With the fragrance of wheat stalks
  And orange blossom.
We shall call the honored guests
To the grass and children's festival,
And thank our good supporters
  And steadfast free men,
The arches of grey hair and memories;
Remember our departed loved ones,
Open widely our doors for the winds,
And establish a science university
  And open a school for struggle.

  We may now reclaim the gold
  And recover the store of wrath
To the Arab treasury.
We may now remember our forefathers
And the details of our heritage,
And speak of wheat stalks and chemistry,
Retrieve the alphabet
And remember we were born in the past
On the mercy of God and prophets;
  And that we were born in the past
On the wrath of God.
  From one ordeal, the will pushed us to another.
We were born by experience,
One generation like another in grief.
We were born for death,
Slowly, propagating in us.

Familiar prayers disavowed us;
The exiles grudged us an atonement.
The stones took us from our shame
And carried us, far beyond the sins.
And in the fire purgatory
We repented to God and land.
Before the mirror flames,
We divulged all our secrets,
All that the hopes have hushed.
God shouted to us, "Be," and we were.
And God ordered, "Return," and we returned.
From a thousand losses we were found,
From a thousand deaths we were born.
We were promised, and we returned.
In a thousand nights and calamities,
    We promised
To give the streets the names of those
Who did not walk on them for long
(Because the way of martyrdom was the way).
The steps of our lifetime decided to walk
(The steps of their lifetime decided to flow).
We'll give the streets
The names of those
Who did not walk on them for long.
We'll give our olive groves the fruit
That has always been difficult and impossible,
And call the start after the start:
Ugly patience! Fine patience!
We'll preach miracles in the land,
A martyr, returning a new day,
A gentle child, a grave old man,
An age greeting an age.
One generation paying homage to another.
We'll plait a rainbow out of lightning,
And grow roses with lightning,

For the names of our future children.
We'll carry our children round our necks
On our feast mornings.
We'll greet in all languages,
All the humans
(Welcome to Palestine!
Brokheem haba'eem l'Falesteen
Welcome to Palestine!
Dobra pajalovat vam v plestin!)
Yes, and we'll groom the fate anger.
Yes, and the destination horses.

The parents' satisfaction is a slim possibility.
The roses have withered among the old graves.
The dust silence has spread on them.
Of the grace of our forefathers,
Speak a generation bartering one time for another.
We did our best and burned in a little light.
Ashes piled on us.
The phoenix date is a moment outside time.
But she will come.
The parents' satisfaction is probable.
We are not experts on despair.
We give a little bread and salt.
We give the hope that has remained with us,
And shake off some of the travel dust.
A female martyr's meal is enough
        For two male martyrs.
Welcome, welcome,
Welcome, our folks!
The hard is easy.
And welcome to our expected birth.

Here we give a breeze to our times' turns.
We contemplate the edge's roses,
Laden with fire and shame.
We stare at its barbed wires
And wash in the mine hole our perished desires.
Here we are yesterday,
Here we are today,
And all the roads to our tomorrow lead.
All who were gone will soon return
To a heap of soil,
And all who died will soon return
To a page in a book,
To a palm tree birthday,
To the morning coffee,
The home, the neighbor,
To a sweet sitting at a door.
Yes, returning,
To a cup of water, gently spilled on a jasmine stalk,
To the graduation of the pride of girls
And the grace of boys.
Yes, returning, indeed returning,
To a holy start,
To a wheat stalk,
To a rose in the waste,
To the work of digging up secrets
In a deserted orange grove;
To the lilies of the wild in the remains of alcoves,
To embracing and kissing,
To whispering and touching,
To candles and tears
After the absence . . . the absence . . . the absence!
"Yes,"
Returning,
"Sure,"
Returning,

"Yes indeed!"
Welcome, oh welcome
To our wedding first,
To our sun first,
To order Quds first,
Welcome, oh welcome!
With white,
Black,
  Green,
Red,
The female martyr's meal is enough
For two male martyrs.
And God is greater!
God is greater!
God is greater!

(pp. 73–95)

3

I'll Get Out of My Image One Day
(2000)

A Palestinian Love Song

Alienation, away from your hands, kills me.
And kills me the yearning in your eyes.
So, spread out the wind carpet,
A *kufiyyah*, woven of my wounded homeland.
To fly,
No barrier, no police, no permits,
To fly me to you;
For I am pining . . .
Pining.
Yearning in your eyes kills me!
I called . . .
Who are you?
You are not my dream boy,
Not a film star
On whose image I reveal my love.
You are not a cavalier image
Who comes on his steed
From the fantasy world.
I called . . .
Why you?
You are the one who had my back
In the face of the Army,
And saved me from their gas
With your scented handkerchief.
You bandaged my wound
With lilies.
And on my forehead, you healed my burns.
With you I became stronger,
With me you became greater,
And I am pining . . .
Pining.
Yearning in your eyes kills me.
So, spread out the wind carpet,

A *kufiyyah*, from my wounded homeland;
To fly me from the *Buraq* Wall,
   From Christ's resurrection,
To fly me, to you . . .

~~~

Let me smell the home basil on your forearms.
Let me rest my cheek on your palms;
Because I love you,
And I love you.
My heart pulses in you,
Your heart pulses in me,
And I love you . . .
Oh, you, streets' hurricane,
Squares' wrath,
Banners' flame,
Desire of greenery in the fields;
Oh, pain of the camps,
Discerned, in the burst of the veiled.
Oh, lilies' smile in the garden of tears,
Pining, I am pining,
Yearning in your eyes kills me.

~~~

Spread out the wind carpet,
A *kufiyyah* woven of my wounded homeland,
To fly,
No barrier, no police, no permits,
To fly me to you,
   To fly me, to fly me,
To you.

(pp. 16–19)

Our Café

A day ago, an hour, a minute,
Twenty years ago,
Our café was a wing dreaming in the clouds.
Among the crowd of customers we had
Two chairs, flowers, and Youth.

A day, an hour ago, a blink of eyelashes,
Twenty years ago,
 A lily nested in our café corner.
 It sprinkled its fragrance in our palms.
We were taken by a daze,
Between two cups,
Smoke branches and fog butterflies.

Twenty years later,
Snatched me from the chronic life details
Memories, of a turgid moment.
Snatched me, towards our café.
But I could not find it.
I wish . . . I wish . . . I had not returned to it.
It was no longer a nest on the cloud branch.
It became a garment boutique.

(pp. 33–34)

No Use

You say, "I am returning" . . .
And the lightning snatches you from me.
Between one sorrow and another
I say, "He will return from the cold exile,
To the warmth of my lap."
But . . . no use!

I say, "I am returning,"
And the waves snatch me from your arms.
Between my sorrow for myself,
And my fear for you,
I say, "I am returning,
To press my heart on your lips."
But . . . no use!

I wished your shade were a house
On some obscure hillock,
In one of its balconies
You would expect an epic poem,
Inspired by me, alone.
Between a cup and one after,
Between a cup and a kiss,
And a flutter of a bee
On a promising flower;
Between the house and a new one
Before the end of song,
    I set the table for you.
You carry me in your arms, to bed,
With the incoming night.
I wished with all my heart,

With all my sorrow, yearning, dread,
I wished . . . but no use!

⸺

May God help you! How you were chased
By roads beyond the roads,
Behind your stray gazelle!
May God help me! Besieged by many hearts
Around my dying hearth.
May God help us! Two faces, the exile is the same.

⸺

You say, "I'm returning."
I say, "I am returning."
We say, "Life may become kind,
As everything is probable."
We say, my love, we say, we say,
We say, but there is no use.
No use!

(pp. 39–42)

A Section of Interrogation Minutes

— And how do you call the homeland?

— My homeland.

— Then you confess?

— Yes, sir, I do confess.

I am not a professional tourist!

— You say my homeland?

— I say my homeland.

— And where is my homeland?

— Your homeland.

— And where is your homeland?

— My homeland.

— And the thunderbolts?

— My horse neighing.

— And the storming winds?

— My extension.

— And the fields of fertility?

— My effort.

— And the mountains' grandeur?

— My self-esteem.

— And how do you is call the homeland?

— My homeland.

— And how do I call my homeland?

— My homeland.

(pp. 57–58)

Departure Poem
For the Political Refugees in Europe's Cafés

A language, whose forefathers' birthplace
Is a homeland,
Claiming another homeland,
Whose forefathers' birthplace
Is a different language.
A language claiming a homeland;
Claiming a homeland where nothing is read,
Except bowing before the imperative:
"Give and produce for us."
We are the masters of land and weather,
We order in the name of iron,
Inscribe by fire our names on the skin of the newborn.
We came with the light of new time,
For you to see us in your mirrors.
We are the civilization.
We are the punishment and salvation.
So be, when you can be,
The way the bullets like you to be.
      A language claiming a homeland
That cannot well pronounce its foreign accent,
And does not relish its officers' jargon,
Cannot stand its rifles, and its soldiers breaking
Into a peaceful home.
There is no escape, then, from a warm, wrathful blood.
No escape.
A language claiming a homeland,
A homeland rejects,
A nation rising;
The brigades of its wound's alerts,
In the civilized darkness, are eyes that do not wink.
On every door the hand of terror hangs a gallows' rope.
For every mouth there is a despot's lock.

The siege is two sieges:
The military barrier has two directions,
Two deaths for despair,
Two faces for death;
The violated homeland has but one face,
One only.
It was inevitable,
To take a step backwards,
For the wind arrow
To miss a neck rising from dark caves,
To pinnacles attracting the morn.
It was inevitable,
To take a step backwards,
Until direction lines assume
The texture to suit
The banner's grandeur.
It was necessary for the faithful messengers
To emigrate,
To prepare what they could . . .
They had to cross.
The crowd was heavy on the bridge,
The weather unsettled,
The roar of waters,
Laden with victims' silence.
They had to cross.
Around them were invaders' spies,
Behind them informers, who take a shred
Of their shirts
For the police dog to sniff.
Around them a constant danger,
Imminent and fierce.
They had to cross the country
To a refuge.
They had to avoid the fog,
     And pulse of fear.

They had to cross, with messages
From their leaders,
And their wives' supplications.
Their children were asleep,
They bent over their necks,
They checked the heat of their kisses.
Their hearts avoided
A cause for weeping.
So they will not gaze for long,
On the sleeping young faces.
They will not take a long goodbye.
It's time to manage a good escape.
They checked their sorrow
With prophetic gravity
And veiled themselves with prayers,
And a head kerchief of darkness.
They went on their immigration nowhere,
Under the guide's arm.
Their destinies
But the mercy of God, and the night,
Are wide.
The exiles were ready
With the cafés of old Europe,
For the end of the echo,
And the beginning of the talk.

It was inevitable for them to cross.
They crossed, swearing by their exile
To return triumphant,
Or martyrdom will be their lot.
After long exile and journey's fatigue,
They crossed, dreaming of their houses' doors,
        And resorted to destiny's door.
Their exile ink was between their eyelids.

In Europe's old cafés
Their prophecies dawned on them.
They ploughed the white paper
And heaped their madness seeds in words
Arranged by sorrow and fear
Letter after letter.
They wept to their fingers.
Around them is a language
They cannot speak,
And stupefied waiters.
        Every now and then
They were saved by a friend,
Just starting his exile.
Foreign police used to besiege him
In his house. But an old woman
Opened a secret door for him,
Which, in Ottoman times, was his father's refuge,
When the soldiers surrounded the house,
To draft the deserter boy, to the war.
How did you leave the homeland?
How is the people's patience
In facing the locust?
Did you see the companions, before you left?
My sick mother is killed by my exile,
My father . . . a patient man,
But the family needs, my friend,
Pull down the mountains;
And fear of hunger,
My companion, is a disgrace;
The foreigner rule, a chronic disease.
Oh well, companion,
Our blood is a bridge
Between one state and another.

In Europe's cafés they met:
A university student, from Cairo;
A teacher, followed by spies' eyes
In Jerusalem and Nazareth,
A mosque speaker from Damascus,
Chased by the foreigner;
    A young artist, deprived of her Iraq's palm trees;
A yarn worker, a steel plant worker from Morocco,
A Libyan revolutionary girl,
An intellectual
Who learned from Lebanon cedar
What the vibrant language said,
And a poet from the Gulf.

In Europe's cafés
They met between a wound and another
They lighted their pains with chaste tears.
There is no escape from or draw.
Oh, no escape from our purifier.
They desired the café with cardamom,
The firebrands of oak wood.
They desired the shout *yahala*, welcome.
They rejoiced with the letters of their loved ones,
And cried, dreaming of their return,
In coffins, or hoisting their banners
To the glory of heavens and earth.
They gathered their sorrow,
But divided the loaves among themselves.
Worried by love, dreams, death, knowledge,
They mastered all accents
As they mastered
The pavement's accent.
Burned by their memories

And yearning for homes,
Which were not helpful in love.
They blessed their nights with chants
About the love of Qais and Layla,
About the unjust exile,
Of the lovers.

Oh, night, do not deter the wanderers
From unknown destinations.
O, night,
Let them repeat their chants
The way they like.
Suffice for them that they
Left their details at home.
Suffice for them that they
Are here and nowhere.
Suffice for them that they
Look like their features
In the mirrors,
Parallel to themselves.
But they left their details
At home
And borrowed a mask for departure.
They borrowed the steps.
They borrowed the road.
Much consolation is behind little consolation.
The heart of the guide
Is still the guide.
From Europe's cafés
To a house in Upper Egypt,
To a house in Hijaz,
To a house in Galilee,
Suffice for them that,
Whenever a little girl

Was playing near them,
They remember another girl,
In the remote, orphaned homeland.
Whenever a balcony was lighted, in the exile
Their emotions were stirred by a balcony
Weeping, in their houses, at home.
Whenever they glimpsed a bird
In the remote evening
They recalled the sparrows in their orchards,
In the orange groves of their neighbors,
And recalled their bleeding, love legends.
Whenever, in their exile gardens,
A rose opened,
The dormant stab in their ribs opened.
Whenever a woman smiled for them,
In their eyes laughed a brook
Of the obstinate vineyard passion,
Generous with its ready tears.

Never absent from their hearts
Was a homeland laughing in every feast,
Frowning under its fetters.
On a horizon, where the dry trees are green,
Never absent was a joy
At the arteries burning
In the despot's prison,
Whose heart is his black prison.
Never absent from their hearts
A joy, whose color was snatched,
By a tear.
When they learned that some companions
Were bribed, and they betrayed,
They regretted the setbacks of their childhood,
They regretted their seats in their school days,

Their dream of a free homeland.
Something like death hovered
Over their bread and salt.
The hearts were disturbed,
So they resorted to some wise madness,
And they did not fall.
And was not absent from them
A miserable joy,
Not absent from them a tear
Whose desperate salt was alien
To their salt.

~~~

A night craving for the day,
A day yearning for its night.
The time is not the time their exile hours know.
Minutes overstep their years.
The seconds are seasons.
Heat and cold have a fever and a swoon.
Oh, night, dear night!
Let down on a quiet dream
The eyelashes of an alien,
Exhausted by nightmares.
Oh, night, dear night!
Remote is home
Handkerchiefs are bleeding,
And consolation is remote, remote.
The weeping of the alien
Is obstinate consolation.

~~~

It was inevitable for them to cross once,
They crossed twice.
Their coffins rested, and their banners rested,
Leaving us a thousand, thousand debts.

I am their banners' child,
Their objectives' son
And I am in between.
I am standing at your luxurious doors
Oh, Europe's cafés. Look,
Do you see in my features
The exile of my old men?
Look, do you see
The ancient yearning
To the homeland of excessive ordeals?

You have my abundant gratitude;
You have entertained
My people's rebels, my abundant wrath.
You have entertained the planners
Of my murder in those cafés
And formulated your costly joke.
Oh, Europe's cafés, look
Oh, Europe, remember,
They crossed the bridge. . . . Try now to cross
Try to divulge the secret of your sins.
They returned from death, with death.
They returned from the memories that did not die.
So, remember them . . .
They returned, so get up and atone
For your sins. Get up, then, and atone.
They crossed . . . they crossed . . . they crossed . . .
It is time for you to cross.
Atone,
And cross, Europe, cross.

(pp. 104–15)

Fantasy

I'll strip off the admiral's badge and rank,
Dismiss the death squad,
No more princes after today,
No execution of princes.
I'll sow my mines throughout God's land,
And sow my tunes,
To reap this scanty wheat of the land,
Between the Nile and the desert,
And offer that wheat
To the Bedouin women of Sinai,
To the miserable people of Sudan.
I'll collect dates from the Euphrates Valley
And feed the poor.
I'll present a gift to the Moroccan West:
Some letters from the Jerusalem book,
Laden with fragrance,
From Damascus groves.
On doomsday, I should have enough mediation
For killing one monster a day,
        From the monsters of this world,
Carousing, between the gulf and the ocean.
Suffice that with a Molotov cocktail
I can burn all the oil in the belly of the earth,
And all the rancor, in the belly of man.
Suffice that I offer a mouth and hand,
To the torture of poetry and poets,
And save the dictionary innocence
From the brothel of speech.
So no Franks can adulterate with it,
Nor with it the Magi talk nonsense.
I, the haunted with the dead and wounded,
I, the dedicated to dreams,
In eloquent Arabic.

Welcome, welcome!
Nurse Halimah rescued me once more,
And said to me with a blessing:
      Cross over the land of God, in the name of God.
Hoist the desert banner
Over things and names.
And she said to me, with a blessing:
You will strip off the admiral's badge and rank,
And dismiss the death squad.
No more princes after today,
No execution of princes.

I'll strip both the admiral,
His badge and rank;
Dismiss the death squad,
And hoist the old Arab banner,
      From the Moroccan West
To Egypt's Kinanah valley,
Crossing over to Hijaz land,
To the land of the Two Rivers,
To the Levant.
And execute the death squad.

                                        (pp. 123–26)

— 4 —

*Funeral Oration by the Deceased
at His Memorial Celebration (2000)*

At His Memorial Celebration
A Flock Poem

Now, it is my pleasure to express my abundant gratitude,
From all my strong heart,
To all the delegations that poured from distant lands
To escort my poor remains;
To all who afforded my coffin a smooth journey,
On their wide shoulders . . .
To all those who bought me wreaths
Of flowers slow to wither.
And what should I say
To that whom my life disturbed
And my death disturbed her disturbance!
To her who wept so much for me
Until the tears her makeup spoiled?

And what should I say
To the grief roses, and the stupor thorns,
To the faces' wax, the elegy coal, the drums' fire?
If I forget, I would not forget
Those who cut short their vacation for me,
And came to honor my poor person
With the strength of this funeral,
Those who sent condolence telegrams,
Those who made condolence telephone calls,
Those who broke in tears,
Those who refreshed my ashes with prayers.
May God requite and bless you all.
And, then, you
By the Will of the Sublime, the Great,
The Omnipotent, the Compassionate,
Are following in our steps,
To Paradise, or Hell.

We are for Him, to Him, as usual, returning.

    Yes, I treacherously died.

And I ask death permission to thank the treacherous stab,

And plant in the wound's balcony a rose for your sake,

To diffuse fragrance for you, and reveal what the waist bleeds,

And postpone the death of butterflies for a day,

To look down upon doomsday.

O my friends,

Of my death and my father's death,

The pious and trustworthy chroniclers

    May say whatever they want.

In my mother's wedding

There is great clarity.

In the husband, my uncle

There is great obscurity.

And here I am, a fully grieved orphan,

Who sees a figure in the fog.

I address him but he answers not.

I draw my sword and shout:

Who are you? Who are you?

You who besiege me with shadows,

And grab the mystery for a while, then escape,

And I grab it for a while, then it escapes,

You who stir under the calm of the ashes

    The clatter of the question?

Be kind to Hamlet.

Be kind to Hamlet.

Painfully, the war looked like war,

O, my friends, painfully looking like friends,

The sudden peace was a twin to all wars;

And it looked like peace,

Painfully, the speech reclaimed speech
And there is no consolation,
But a flitting figure from the old castle's fog,
    Warning me of the day,
Recommending me to the Angel of Darkness.
Around me close
My doubts and my folk's phantoms
The jaws of siege set in
Without an arm to support my back,
    Without a wall.
In a thousand chaotic states,
I turn on my chaotic pivot,
And turn my chaos upside down,
Arrange my sorrow prayers,
What you and I did.
And I remember that my ribs
Have become twins with my prison bars.
And I remember how I tattooed my arm
With a naked beauty, shaded by my sail,
Dreaming, dreaming how she would become
My compass, in my loss.
And I remember how I drew, on my death horizon,
A swallow, and I drew the spring
On my house door.
And I remember how I forgot the frost,
How I forgot a wing, lost on a tree of clouds,
Lost.
And I remember how I remembered that I forgot,
How I forgot, and how
I remembered that I remembered that I forgot,
And how I die because I live,
And how I live because I die.
Sometimes, I am invaded,
By Hamlet's pains,
And Hamlet's sorrows,

And Hamlet's ghosts,
Then I escape

I am the man of fire.
The north wind steals my ashes,
So I walk on the brands.
I believe, I believe. Here I clasp the wind brand,
And here I clasp the brand a cold on my sigh,
And peace on my bewilderment.
Of late I believed all speech.
Today I believe not to believe anything,
Of fire and snow.
How can I believe my father's death,
And the mythical marriage of my mother to my uncle?
How can I believe this fog, this mirage, this waste?
And how can I believe that I am free,
When my fetters chew on my nerves.
And grind my bones?
I'm the man of fire and snow.
The fire is not mine. The snow is not mine,
Waking is not mine. Dreaming is not mine.
All dust.
And dust I am. My father, where are you?
And where is my refuge, my mother's chest,
My mother's soul! I am your son, Hamlet.
Your husband is not my father.
My father, where are you?
I call you from the depth of my sorrow and fear,
My orphanhood and weakness.
Bring me, bring me a handful of desert sand
(Before the discovery of aircraft carrier fuel)
Bring me a gulp of impure water, discharged by the Nile,
A drop of water grudged by the Turkish brothers,
A drop of mud oozed by the Tigris and the Euphrates.

Hamlet's heart is dying of thirst.
But there is no loving father,
No mother shedding a tear of fear
And hug, at the moment of death, Hamlet's sorrows,
And Hamlet's corpse.

⟶

Farewell, farewell, dear kingdom of Denmark.
I know that the Mafia will murder me in my bed,
At dawn, without my coffee,
For a dangerous suspicion that I was born to live.
But I swear I am innocent,
Innocent. I have no illusions.
I realize that I was born for the Mafia
To assassinate me, while asleep and dreaming.
But my question is: why my assassination,
When I have not yet committed the crime
Of taking even one sip of cardamom,
　　With my morning coffee?
I ask, pardon my asking,
Why am I assassinated
For a simple dream,
Which bordered with my sleep?
Why my assassination
Before taking a shower
With a little water dropped by the dream,
From a cloud of imagination?
Why . . . why my assassination?
For a shadow to be born of my shadow,
And grow up, starting from my morning,
To live in my house,
Burn my house with my fire . . .
Why?!

⟶

And here I am, thanking you abundantly.
It is my pleasure that I can read
My obituary in the newspapers.
It is my pleasure to see these tables set on my name.
It makes me laugh to hear all this fly buzzing,
This theatrical grief,
This "ado and no flour,"
The tapping on song tambourines,
And the beating on poems' drums.

My elegy is easy,
But my death is difficult.
Yes, I know that I have now become
     A bull, without horns.
My back is stabbed by one matador after the other,
While beautiful women, in the balconies,
Wave to the courageous matador
Knocking down an old sorrowful bull.
So, forgive me:
My elegy is easy.
My death, difficult.
I still retain what may curtail directions,
Some dreams and memories,
And a willow combing in the wind,
An olive tree, remembering God in the house yard.
On the wall there are still
Some family pictures
And a double flute that I cannot play well,
But it can play well,
When the evening breeze
Blows into its lips.
My elegy is easy,
My death, difficult.

The sky mirrors are my mountains,
My plains are the mirrors' mirrors.
The homelands' mirrors are my homeland,
The mirrors, I look into them for a long time.
I see the faces of all homelands and all nations,
I see every race except me,
My homeland is the mirrors.
I look into them for a long time,
I see the Gauls, the Huns, the Persians,
The Franks, the Indians, Gog Maggog,
Humans, Jinns, White, Black, Yellow, Red.
        The face is not mine,
The hands are not mine.
Mirrors!
Mirrors!
My homeland is the mirrors.
        I gaze into them, I gaze for long.
I see everything,
Except myself.

Whereto does the dwindling expanse lead?
To where is this departure-residence,
This boring turning round?
The home is not a home,
The people not the people.
The wound does not doze,
Nor does the heart forget,
Or life pardon,
Or death attract.
Whither this going-returning, presence-absence,
Mirage, waste, torment?
A door, without a wall,

Becomes a wall, without a door.
And what remains: depart, depart, depart.

Let my grief hurricanes fall on death castle.
Let volcano whims curtail the geography
Of replete-void,
And the rites of ceremonies,
    And seasonal speeches.
Let darkness caves set loose the wading horses.
Bring me your unruliness as light and fire,
You God's curse,
    And spread your sash,
You God's mercy,
I am not the earth Atlas,
Not the earth Atlas.
    Who am I to bear the miserable land of madness?
Lonesome, vagrant, outcast,
With a bladeless sword, a nation but no people,
Alive and dead, and alive and dead,
On the green square of the barbarian
    Nations Organization.
Let my grief hurricanes
    Fall down on the death castle,
And let death cut it short.

I was ordered to obey them.
I did not barter dear for cheap.
I obeyed the Prophet, and the authorities.
I lived and died, and lived and died
On the law of God and love,
    Secretly and openly.
I showed my steady torment sedately,
And when the answer was involved,

In the question chaos,
I resorted to the ancients' wisdom.
I was never very impatient with complaining "Ah!"
Even when the Ah was impatient
I was never impatient with God's lot.
I became addicted to my stupor,
Learned wisdom by my consciousness,
Kept my limits, without limits,
Suffering pain, beyond the body limits.
Under my ashes, kindled my grief,
There lie brands bequeathed by grandfather
To a father, appealing to son,
And from a son floating in the space of times,
Exploding in the haze,
Towards the progenies' wish,
One generation after another,
Until eternity decides.
There is no place where to rest my place,
And no time to measure the ages of my travels by,
And to adjust its loose hours,
    And count minutes.
Around me are millions. Around me are millions;
    Around me, but none is there, none is there.

I bless. I curse. I believe. I disbelieve. I believe.
There must be an energy in the sky of tin.
There must be a glitter in the icy weather
To melt the mythical snow,
To grow new grass on the roof of my house,
For a swallow to build her nest
In the cracks of my last wall.
My soul was fluttering over the deep.
I often said to my soul,
Out of darkness will come light,

And it will be called day,
And our Creator will bless His creation,
And out of the rock will come roses,
There will be wheat stalks,
There will be births,
And God will be pleased with us.
I said to my soul,
There will be a tomorrow,
And it will be yesterday for a new day.
From every race a couple would be saved on the Ark.
    Noah will be happy.
And we will be happy when we kiss our parents
On the faces of our children.
The mythical snows will melt.
She said, when, how, where?
I calmed my soul.
My wounds fraternized my wounds.
    I said, we shall start where we started
    And start where we ended.

I deserted my father's palace, regrettably.
And I deserted my father's palace without regret.
Between my prudent madness
And frightful mind, I read the book of storms.
And I realized. I realized that I am a captive
Of the incessant question, and that I am
Sunk in the depth of the puzzle:
"To be" (as life would want me!),
"Or not to be" (as museums would claim me!).
I deserted my father's palace frightened.
And I deserted my father's palace not frightened.
I deserted the palace, the throne of rubies and scepter,
To build me, from my defiance,
A palace, a throne, time honored and new,

Standing in water,
Verdant in the earth,
Alive and free, fresh of songs.
White in hope, with open skies.
I deserted, deserted, deserted,
My father's palace with no regret.

When shall the earthquakes' gazelle rest?
Where shall the storm's eagle hang his flooded shirts?
And where shall the martyr's heart,
And liberty fighter's face
Restore some of his characteristic marks?
And how can the catastrophe
Express its names with the needed clarity?
How can the lies speak of their real desire?
And how can I win the secret of nature and beings,
When there is no secret left . . .
And around me, wherever I turn,
Is the wall of myths.
        Around me, the traps of paronomasia,
The jelly of antonomasia,
Before and after?
Around me, in honor of death
The people of life set up their banquets,
Drunk, they dance; sing among graves.
They give their dead a remnant drink
That gives no longer life, or shorter one.
When can I rest?
And where can my silence reign?
Or where can I shout?
After the Last Supper, was I Judas?
Or did they crucify me because I am Christ?
I tried, learned, unlearned, and asked,
Am I Hamlet or Samih?

I tried, tried,
Can I have your mercy bullet,
You good brothers?
And who of you would offer me
A cigarette alms, and a final hope,
And comfortable death,
So the ashes will be forgotten,
And the wind will remember?
I tried, tried,
When shall I rest, when shall I rest?

Under the foggy wing, I see some steeds
Galloping, with armored cavaliers.
But there is no neighing, and no rustling, none.
In the height of the sun I hear a clatter,
Of a huge crowd,
The roar of regiments shakes my incited blood.
I call from the depth of my heart:
Get up my bride, get up my Jebus,
Get up, they are coming.
Prepare roses for their ranks, and rice!
But they disappear.
There are no ranks, no swords,
No bride, no Jebus,
No faces, no suns, no shades, none.
I shout, "Ophelia, rescue me!
Take my hands to your shoulders,
My face in your palms.
Lift me to you . . . lift me!
Perhaps I could see what I hear,
And hear what I see;
Witness the growth of what I sowed,
And the revelation of what I hide.
Perhaps I could believe or disbelieve!"

Why did I give her an appointment outside time?
How did I dare crush her rose under my foot,
When she ran away, barefoot,
From her father to meet me!
Why did I turn away when they pointed at her,
With a bloody incriminating finger,
"She is the adulteress!"
"She is the adulteress!"
How can I atone for the purity of this question
When all their answers are wrong?
And how can I train my obstinate skull?
Let thunderbolts strike my forehead.
Let the lightning snatch me
To the other shore of eternity.
My heart connived against me
With grief and doubt.
My heart colluded.
My blood serpents were about to devour me.
My steps kept away from my steps.
Whither should I go?
No road could lead.
Whither should I go
        With my grief, horror, resentment?
Whither shall I go?

I felt thirsty.
I had no mirage drink except Ophelia's tears.
I felt hungry.
I had nothing but this god of dates.
All right. Dates and tears.
Soon I will feel very hungry
But there is no food except my wedding feast.

All right. My roses and oil,
And what is left of my dough.
I'll try later not to feel hungry.
I'll try to help my thirst with my tears.
I'll let myself begin
With killing the bats.
I hate these bats, stuck to my ribs.
I hate this darkness, fond of killing my candles.
I felt thirsty. I felt hungry.
From my body is their bread.
From my blood is their wine.
They fought me with Ophelia.
They besieged me with her.
They do not like her.
They do not like me.
Do I love miserable Ophelia?
Does beautiful Ophelia love a cavalier of smoke?
A prince without sway or scepter?
I love?
She loves?
The question remains:
To be—as imagination flight wants me,
And not to be—the dust of Time
        Beyond the void of place?

Ophelia may resent my prudent madness.
She may suspect me.
She may suspect my suspicion.
She may fear.
And resort to curse me, by yearning
For a man she may finally rest on his chest.
But Ophelia's luck is miserable.
Around her are the elite of the homeland dignitaries,
Of the struggle poets and locust savants,

She is besieged by a battalion of men
    Without chests. She has no chest but mine.
Ophelia has no other lovers but me,
No other mad men but me.
I adore, adore Ophelia.
When I say I love you, Ophelia weeps and laughs.
She weeps on me, and weeps on her,
And I drown in Ophelia's tears.
Ophelia was transformed to mirrors by mirrors.
I gaze in them for long,
And see mountains in them,
And plains,
And see all nations and all faces but me,
But me, but me!
I weep, and the mirrors weep.

The kingdom of Denmark has its will . . .
To let the rot diffuse
And plague the country's heart
And the spirit of the nation,
Or restore the fragrance of the homeland.
And I have my will to let out my secret,
My good and evil.
I, the last rebel, the free captive,
    The wretched prince,
I, the Arab Hamlet, witness me:
Training my mind in the madness puzzles.
My father is dead, who does not die,
    My mother is my mother.
My kingdom is booty for my uncle.
I have a phantom in the fog.
Insisting with no speech,
"The kingdom is yours . . . the kingdom is yours."
And I demand my kingdom!

To wipe off my kingdom's face
All the darkness and dust.
    But at the peak of my fear for her,
And grief for myself,
I am surprised at the height of the moon by a night
Rattling my bones in the frosty waste.
I raise my sword eastwards,
But neighs in the West,
A guffaw of the victorious over my people's graves,
And my dead, fall around me.
I raise my sword westwards
But the East dagger stabs my side.
A palm tree falls out of my hold at Baghdad Gates.
I hold a minaret in the fog of death.
I appeal to Al-Hussein,
But my hands are severed from Cairo's hands.
I hold, I lose. I hold. They loosen.
And I swoon, and fall in the palace yard.
Hamlet falls in the palace yard.

       ⟞⟝⟝⟝

Far away am I. Far away is the spring,
I know I am far away from the spring,
I know what the thirst wants.
But I don't know.
I crept on sand, and rocks, and snow,
And brands, and thorn, and pining,
And doubt, and yearning . . .
What does the thirst want?
    I crept, my skin was worn,
My flesh was worn out.
My bones covered with rust.
I know I am far from the spring,
I know I am near to death.
What does thirst need?

I have no winter, no summer.
I have no sword, and no conqueror.
My homeland flesh and mine
Was scattered all over,
Was turned all over.
Then let thirst be what it wants
And what I did not want.
And you, death, unsheathe
The swords of drought on Hamlet's neck,
For Hamlet to rest in death,
Hoping the spring will one day bring
A resurrection for Hamlet.

⟿

My darkness is dubious
Ophelia cannot believe.
Now, it is my pleasure
To express my abundant gratitude,
From all my strong heart,
To all the delegations
    That poured from distant lands,
To escort my poor remains.
To all who afforded my coffin a smooth journey,
On their wide shoulders.
To all those who bought me wreaths
Of flowers slow to wither.
To suit this decline
And what should I say?
What should I say?
What should I say?
What should I say?
What . . . ?

(pp. 5–60)

~ 5 ~

Atlantis King (2003)

A Flock Poem

My throne is on water. My kingdom is on water . . .
And of water are my scepter subjects.
Risking my innocence . . . I prepared the fire baptism
And passed through hell towards the torment
Of the first Paradise.
I shook my last illusion off my hands.
I salvaged the water throne from my sinking ships;
Lifting my face to the sun of minutes and seconds,
King, installed by seaweeds,
Despite the short time,
Followed by storms, ships, and songs,
King over Atlantis' desires,
Asking for another foothold,
        In the orb of space.
I walked, supported by water glory,
Pleased . . . for defeating hunger
Of a million, by five loaves.
I reveal: live fishes slipped out
Of the old fishing gear in the oppressive seas.
A king, over the Atlantis of desires, was my will.
For every color, a rose.
And for every sound, a song.
For every foothill a breeze,
Laden with salvia dew,
        Washed by valley tears.
A hope for every dawn,
A king then . . . in his water palace,
With a retinue of steam.
At his pining limits,
Are towns swarming with people
Coming from seashells.
His armies come and go the way they like,
To wherever they like,

And come back with pearls,
Slave girls, jewels and gold.
A king, newly familiar with the world,
And the cycle is disturbed.
Grass prayers in the Balkans wither.
Flock bells ring in the contaminated clouds.
The country songs in Caucasia are silent.
In Chernobyl expanse phantoms are asleep.
Here is the other Chernobyl
That dies and does not die.
And here, death dust is celebrating
     The pigeons' nests.
A king then, I say to me,
A king. . . . Your embroidered robe
Is not helpful supplication.
Leave the subjects in peace.
Go to the violet sorrow,
And settle as pollen on tulip corolla.
Oh, you, coming on sand ebb,
And departing with the wind's flow!
The tale's lot is that its end
Should be the beginning of the end.
Neither Scheherazade nor a morning!
Atlantis bathed in your tears.
And you bathed in its water,
Between reality and sleep.
Sleepwalk then, sleepwalk,
And tour in a white robe
Throughout the town.
Walk on its walls as a phantom,
From the glare of palaces to the tents.
You may choose, from its halls, a girl,
In the manner of old myths' interest in love.
A king, and the girl from among the people,
In a sudden celebration.

The wind blows, the candles go out.
She hugs him, he hugs her, in a chance darkness.
The light comes back:
He sees her, she sees him.
    And the tale begins.
Roads and balconies are decorated by Atlantis.
Its people come out to dance in the public squares.
This is their national day,
    The people's wedding;
The wedding of his majesty,
Our cherished king.
The end . . . is no end.

The foolish backbite you,
The café's frequenters admire
Another era of history,
    And you are its lawful inheritor.
But the question is the question,
And history's seduction is obvious,
Your face is ambiguous in the shades.
You say it's time . . . your time,
Your bags are not yet ready for departure,
Nor are the farewell handkerchiefs.
Nor is the space settled for you.
Atlantis' limits are getting closer,
The road is not getting longer for you
To change one state for another.
Are you grieved? Don't grieve!
Don't let the bad situation lure your heart
Out of trust in new opportunities.
Oh, me, I-you, still a believer
In God and olives,
Still related to my old, and new books.
I-you still refuse the trick of arbitration.

Some Ash'ari Muslim philosophers
Met me on the roads in the Arena,
Ash'ari Muslim philosophers met me,
I said, I am the decision.
They retreated and ran away
    From the force of revealing proof
And the bright daylight.
A king am I . . .
    Atlantis flourished under my rule.
People's homes are thrifty and safe.
Marvelous fertility is in the land.
How can I accept arbitration?
No, no, this cannot be!
What you claim is a well of madness
No, this cannot be
An excuse for a flood of destruction.

The cosmos is in your hands . . .
You are obsessed by expecting
    Exact appointments.
Oh, wise king!
Nothing is in your hands.
Say nothing will touch you
Except what is written in the old record.
The cosmos is in your hands . . .
    The doors are locked,
And there is no key,
Except the fire needle, in the heap of chaff.
Lightning is striking your bare chest.
The water snakes are snapping at your eyelids,
And there is no swallow.
Oh, disgraced honor. Oh grieved joy!
What should you do?
When the angel is an island,

And the sea is an accursed devil?
What should you do?
When the graves have flowered in the garden,
And the palaces are void of you,
And prisons were hatched in them?
And you may stand on useless ruins
And shed grave tears?

In the corner there is a fireplace with no fire.
Night frost in Atlantis pains
Is death imminent to people.
A fireplace with no fire or firewood
Snow alights in heaps on doors and balconies.
No way out! The voice is your voice,
A moan of the hanged,
In the forgotten noose.
How often you involved your heart
        In the traps of love!
How often you assuaged your obsession
With the affairs of people and revolutions!
A kingdom of rebels—you said to your pure self.
You fraternized contraries in you.
You did not account for weakness and suspicion.
Oh, my face in the mirror!
You did not postpone the bondage
        Of my difficult dream
In the chaos of whims.
Count then, the harvest of illusion,
In a corner with a fireplace,
With no fire, or firewood.
And bite the nails of my suppressed wrath,
Store up the anger,
Perish the hands of my dream,
And perish the dream.

Action!
And the rehearsal begins.
Another round of bullets,
A great show on doomsday,
The great Day of Resurrection.
Cradle and grave,
The earthly space between them is a bed.
Resurrection Day . . . it is Resurrection Day.
The child does not want flowers on the fresh grave,
The wind does not need a fan,
The beginning does not willingly offer
Its dream to whatever the destiny wished.
Action!
The spark blows.
Action!
And civilization goes out.
God's soul returns over the deep,
In a blind eternity.
It is the image of birth after death,
Or it is the state of sudden death,
In its exciting revelation.
You did not play chess well.
Your mate was checked after the first move.
Wish you did not play.
You were tempted to win,
By the losing jugglers,
And you did not win,
So you were defeated. So, defeated,
So, defeated.
And on the remains of the chessboard
You were a loser crucified.
So bear your cross
On the way of thorn and pains

And ascend to the pit.
Many a time you fell to the heights,
A phantom marking time,
Between struggles of existence
And the mazes of evanescence,
Between reality and imagination.
You did not master the chess,
No, you did not master the secret war.
So, go your way,
A chronic goodness in the heart,
Intoxication by hopes and pure intentions.

The sea surface splits, and lo!
A brunette nymph.
In the land of snow they speak of a blonde nymph . . .
Sorry. . . . The Zulu grandma confirms
She was a black nymph . . . a statue of ebony.
You come from multicolor Atlantis,
A memory, a taste, a surprised attitude, no more.
You, the cosmic innovator,
You build the colors' state,
In the name of God, were promised that God
Is merciful, and compassionate.
You forged your crown out of Earth's flowers,
Of golden aspirations to a great love seat.
But it is the colors, you poor
You, haunted by worry,
Split between paradise and hell.
The colors' will refuses the unity of opposites,
In the color of the straight path.
Okay.
Your speech is ambiguous,
Neither dubious nor clear.

Metaphor, metonymy, and sober similes
Are guaranteed by law and etiquette.
Summarize your secret death
By declaring it before your people.
Address the homeland crowds,
Look out of your heart balconies.
A king weakens once . . .
King and a strong man
Who is not good at death, but life
Is stronger by creatures' weakness.
Remember, Master, a being still you are,
A human, your easy is still governed
        By your difficult.
You are the shah, playing with directions,
And you are played by directions.
Okay.
Your speech is clear . . . all right!
Despite the ignorance of the ignorant,
Despite the foolishness of the foolish,
It still turns. . . . The earth still turns.
Some time passes. . . . Water boils in the reservoir
Before the flowing of the falls.
The government meets in the shade limits.
You offered them your soul powers,
You are accused of trusting the riffraff . . .
Assassins, who amicably resort to you,
They hide their weapons in your palace,
Open for visitors.
Tell me, oh, me, the bewitched,
Tell me, have you seen the development of events
Before they happened?
Did you see, or dictate? That is the question.
And over it argument flares.
Did you create Atlantis to drown it,
And create a history lesson;

Or did Atlantis create you,
To drown, in you, the life illusions?
Yes, yes, that is the question,
And over it the argument flares.

Cinema is the change of times,
Circus is the world.
The courageous circus player
Makes the horrible death jump.
Circus then, it is
That assigns the roles to the trainer and lions.
No, no, the circus system is higher;
You are in the chaos of system.
You are at the rush of madness to perdition.
Cinema and circus? No, hell is this world,
Underneath flow rivers,
The lads stretching on flower beds,
Nymphs in the veils of lights.
Honey you like? Milk you desire?
All right! Stick your hands in the rubbish,
Life is short. Life is shorter than an arm length.
There are destinies imposed on you,
        But you never bowed to the wicked storms.
This is how your mother begot you,
Tall, your feet are the despair of ants and worms.
Oh, king of kings!
The blue cloud is your mother.
She begot heaven fertility.
Of holy wind was your father.
So forgive those who betrayed, who disbelieved,
Who sold, who strayed, who lied,
Who ran away, who rejoiced, who trifled,
        Who stole, who deviated, who defied you
        Secretly, and paid you tribute, in public.

Your destiny it was: the collusion of lackeys
And sham characters around your remote seat.
Suffice it is that they witnessed all your deeds.
And with the noble fire flower,
They deceived and fought you,
And blessed and crowned you.
Destiny is imposed on you, and by you.
O, king of time.
Destiny, don't grieve; your stick is a serpent.
Your fiery certitude is censer
      Of misgivings and doubts.
You look out of violent grief;
Do you see anything but torment lemon?
No doubt . . . you miscalculated.
Gold is genuine gold . . .
      And it is not molded of earth.
No doubt . . . you miscalculated.
You equaled your intuition ewes
With the wolves.
You read between the lines,
And did not flatter any letter in the book.
No doubt . . . you miscalculated.
Pay, then, for the mistakes
And go, as going wished.
You lighted a lamp, which went out
Between the night and the wind.
You did not protect it by beating about the bush.
You did not master maneuvering allurement and waste.
Pay, then, for the mistake.
And sink with Atlantis to the bottom pit,
With no return.
No doubt . . . you miscalculated.
Educated rain did not fall on your new farms.
Your pollen wind did not blow.

The Apache helicopter bared the branches.
You shouted from your wrath rags.
The sick Nation Organization did not budge.
You miscalculated . . . yes, you did.
The falling rubble of your roof
      Blocked the last door.
The rubble of your soul besieged the last breath.
Here destiny flings you from destiny to destiny.
No doubt . . . you miscalculated.
You miscalculated. . . . You did.
A king . . . a slave . . . in the fetters of dream,
In disappointments . . . in destructive anger . . .
Master . . . slave. . . . Then, sir
You miscalculated . . . You did.
Around you are numbers . . . arid sand . . . blind.
Your zenith is the kite of sighs,
Rescheduling of debts,
The sin of pacts, self-lashing,
Terrorism. Your knowledge is cursed
By illiteracy, plagues, and lack of dream immunity.
Beneath you is your board,
Encompassed by volcanoes and flood.
Richter is the salvation straw. The scale is set.
Are the measuring gadgets in your hands?
The road maps?
Have you checked the atmosphere in Atlantis?
The weather forecast?
Do you survey public opinion?
Your river is ambiguous.
The people suspect a *Kawthar* river flowing
And a terrible serpent.
Master, your land is good,
Your plant seeds are good,
But the message is tiresome.

The wicked allurement is restive
And on the cross you are nailed and bleeding,
And Deimos is involved in the trial.

⟜

I say to me . . . to say to you
You will return from your exile
Before dying in a new exile,
Drowning, with the happy homeland.
Oh, you resident king, and homeless king,
Poseidon knows what you want,
        And what he wants.
I say to me . . . to say to you
Your palace steps gave the general
His favor with you.
And gave the poets
Their favor with the general.
Atlantis flirts with history favor.
She offers her soul to justice.
The citizen has the right to live
As he likes, with what he likes.
His child has the right to notebooks,
And to reading under electric lights;
The right to the garden green, and medicine.
The general is enticed by the massacre;
He dreams of a military coup.
At the start of the steps,
He bows to a lady, whose breast
Emits lust, and throbs in the exciting corridors
Towards her secret chamber.
Your palace stairs
Are gradually bending towards a pit,
The pit of blood. . . .
I say to me: in the ruby season
The rise of storms will calm down.

You are armed with dreams
Around you regiments of guards keeping watch.
And you dream the way you like,
One hint, and the nymphs of night sea
Are at your service,
Sir, and your plump body is at your service
Your stick is a serpent;
      Its lethal poison responds to your magic.
But it is the hurricane, Master,
Ignorant of guards, constitution,
      And etiquette game,
You are besieged by oppression,
Flood, and blind illiteracy.
How can you tame the crocodile,
      And sudden shark?
You are still in the ruby revolution
The hurricane rage starts on the edges
      Of your kingdom.
The riffraff will emerge from Atlantis shores
And you sink under the surface . . .
Its golden sand will drown in the rushing salt.
The crippled and blind will drown.
The bare feet of runners to the mountains
Are pulled back by the waves.
The riffraff have no escape but to rise to you.
The siege narrows around you.
Waves from the bottom of the ocean
Rage up to you.
The fish lose their school.
The cave octopus clamors in awe.
Dogfish bark in fear.
Whales let off their inner water,
Succumbed to the sea rage.
The foothill trees disappear under the water,
Another wave rises.

Sand and shells cover the roofs and hills,
And sink in the sea weed chaos.
The top of the last mountain whisper
    Dies down in the palace.
In the distance the roars increase!
They have not heard a king singing;
They have seen a king with fire
Raging in his sides as music.
So he burns a capital.
Then he fumbles with the guitar chords,
Squeezing generations' blood in rattling,
And plays in the waking ashes
The dreaming tunes of destruction.
They have not heard a king singing.
Give us, Master, a song
Whose legitimate beauty shines
In the fog of the gloomy steps.
They have not heard . . .
(She left her windows open on my long night,
And left my heart, alone in the darkness.
An icy moon, the night cheats and imprisons
Its sweet light, packed in marble cases.
    She left her windows and disappeared
No farewell, no speech) . . .
They have not heard,
You have not heard.
Atlantis, listen . . . your king is coming out
Of the world of death,
    Celebrating the health of passion.
They have not heard a king singing,
You have not heard a king singing.
Let the red rose be celebrated
    By the bees of love;
And let the horizon clouds be burned
    By pigeon wings.

⌁

It is the crockery ordeal or the granite wisdom,
Oh, king of kings . . .
Easy on a throne rocked
By hidden and open elements,
And give the nature secrets a chance
To reveal, and proclaim.
It's the crockery ordeal of the granite wisdom,
Master, so wake up and beware
At the moment of the great events . . .
And do not bargain with the blight of forgetfulness.
You realize that when dangers congest
How many destinies are in yours.
Oh, you courageous king, oh, you wise king,
Investigate suspicions in Atlantis,
And emerge from the hell of suspicion,
Draped by the paradise of good news.
Do not succumb to the sorrows' will . . .
Light a white candle
Listen to what the grass says;
Listen to the oak trees;
Open the windows of your phantom-haunted palace . . .
Give the wind its chance . . .
Sighs will reach the peak
Their golden age begins
Then the celebration begins
With autumn leaves blown by storms
From the pavement ribs,
With new blood in the arteries of Time
Which pardons Time's halted watches.

⌁

The trees breathe their foliage
And raise their sap promised by the name of God,

To the countryside, the desert, the wells . . .
Stretch out your hands to the poor,
And curtail the limits.
So the being things will be
        The base of your kingdom.
Perhaps, then, the desires' Atlantis
Will be saved from a dying lightning,
        With no thunder.
Oh, you king, crowned by clouds,
        And hearts, and roses. I say to me:
Do not look in the strength of the weak
For an end. Do not trust the weakness
Of the strong. Go to a fire and water
Between Earth and Sky
In the blood-stained castle.
Learn from the weather changes
The ozone has its wisdom,
        Man has his wisdom,
The trees have their wisdom.
The balance of nature
        Is still standing in the earth,
Swung by storms: to stay or perish.
Oh, you besieged king . . .
Beware of laughter besieged by weeping.

You declared the religion of love and realization,
In the name of God.
You addressed the humans by humans.
You brought words back to their objects.
You requested the named to return to its name.
It is inevitable to realize the origins.
You worried . . . I know . . .
Fever touched the springs of your eternal spirit.
I know. . . . Putting the land-home in order

Is still your care, sir, my master.
All over Atlantis the questions are hovering.
Simple people are looking for a solution
For the wheat stalk puzzle.
Bread, my master, is the secret of the problem.
Love and realization are tomorrow's bread.
Today's bread asks for its beginning.
The pests have not yet destroyed all your crop.
Echoes of a song are still wavering on the yellow fields,
And reapers are lying on the straw of death and chaos,
Pregnant women are desiring mulberry and lemon,
On maternity beds.
It is history, Master, who dictates its daily affairs.
The active media follow a moon of cosmic aluminum.
Satellite screens are panting after it.
Do not despair, Master.
      Commercials do not take long,
The news bulletin is following.
You are besieged from the first
To the last piece of news.
War on love, winged with lilies and silk.
War on the dangerous king.
I say to me, to say to you
War is sowing the earth to the orbits
In the wake of blood.
At night . . . the dragon expertise prepares its gear,
And Atlantis's heart whoops.
The wind tightens its raincoat,
And pierces through icy elevations.
At night . . . on the shores is raised the banner
Of new invasion.
Dead and wounded on the roads.
Another wave brings in another wave and returns.
What shall we do?
These walls are weak and cracked,

And about to crumble, and the guards will escape.
Have you prepared, Master, what you cannot
And can do? Have you come out of silk to iron?
A new invasion.
Promising the slave girls with slaves
And I am adjusting the new cravat.
Your royal face, Master, in the mirror . . .
So, come out to the large crowds,
In the captive palace court,
And wake up the ancient dead.
The death of the living is obvious
And scandalous.
The ocean waves are swaying.
The towers are shaking, one stone after another.
What should you do,
You king, besieged by the ruins of the island?
Atlantis apologized to its defense
And your kingdom is in its last moment.

Now, your water's throne sinks.
Waves of darkness cover the feast's joy.
Salinity approaches the kingdom domes.
Another forest drowns.
The green top disappears in the ocean of darkness.
Depths gape open.
The whales' appetite approaches
The cancer procession is stirred
    From its deep holes.
The despair of octopus spreads out
    The trained arms.
Oh, Master, you are in a fatal trap.
In a fatal trap disappear the dense towns
And the isolated villages,
Barracks, temple towers, factories,

Gardens, trees disappear; paved roads,
Ports, cafés . . .
And you remain a captain on the ship tower,
Raising his hands towards God.
Waves collided around you.
The bottom pit is preparing,
        For the great celebration.
Your feet disappear (a captain without feet).
The water rises (a captain without legs).
The water rises. You go down . . .
Your navel is the family celebration,
With the new baby, in the bed.
Your waterbed sinks . . . your palms disappear
Under the water.
Your water head falls,
        Your water hair floats,
On water with no limits,
On water with no limits.
Your spirit is returning to the water.
On the deep it floats.
God recovers His old sign.
Atlantis sinks to the depths.
Kingdom sinks in darkness.
You sink in darkness,
In your adverse daydreams.
And sink the crime secrets.
And sink the crime secrets.
And sink . . .

(October 15, 2002)

6

Visions of Nostrasamihdamos (2006)

Selections from 111 Visions

(1)
      After five decades of death and mourning,
Sindbad returns from his arid voyage
And lights the candles in Baghdad.

(3)
The memory child is born, to a woman from Aswan,
He removes a thousand troubles, quenches every riot;
And the conspiracy fails on the Cairo bridges.
(5)
Before the ripeness of figs and pomegranates,
Ripens in Zaqa, Salt, and Amman,
The fruit of a revelation unto Luke.
(6)
After the silkworm quietly dies, in the mulberry turmoil,
Tyre and Sidon will get up from their stumble,
And Beirut will rest on her throne.
(7)
The wedding folks will rise from their death,
Before sunrise, to dance and sing, and drink,
And the merry around Jerusalem domes.
(8)
After the death rites, return from their diaspora
The people of the land,
The breeze, the smile will return to Kuwait.
(18)
Its foliage deserts her. The desert creeps: death
Over her bare arid regions for sixty months,
Then revives the way she and we like her: green Tunis.
(25)
They clasp the firebrand and raise the banner,
Filling the revolution sky, starting celebrations
In Iskenderun of Arabism and Joy.

(27)

Washington's illusions and those of Rome

Invade people, lands, and stars.

A trip, a fall, a clear fall. . . . Illusion, you won't last.

(32)

On the fourth day of the fourth month of the twenty-fourth century,

The successful businessman from Jenin

Will marry the most beautiful businesswoman, in Berlin.

(37)

On the seventh of September, an educated black lady,

Very tall, will rule America, after serving

Five years and three days at a Navy base.

(42)

The despotic Hebrew king abdicates,

Under senility illusion; and realize the right and wisdom,

And the right path, the children of Israel.

(43)

England is invaded by famine. The people

Revolt against formalities of deceit, fraud, the authorities,

What obedience demands. And the horror in London is over.

(47)

Desertification spreads in the American West and South

Grumbling reaches its peak, to be ended

At the hands of a savior immigrant from Palmyra.

— *7* —

A Very Personal Conversation
with Mahmood Darwish (2009)

A Migration Poem *for Mahmood Darwish*

Beirut has two faces: one for Haifa,
And we are friends, in prison and exile.
We crossed one land after another,
And here we are, returning in the vertigo stutter.
The return pleasure is a quick embrace,
At an airport door.
Was the meeting an apology?
Was the farewell an escape?
Without speech we stretch out the hands.
O my night! O my eye![1]
The night is not a night, nor is the eye an eye.
The Arab world separates us.
     The foreign world joins;
And we remain foreigners in both worlds!
What remains is departure
With the wind from a home in Galilee,
To the wind in a vague hotel,
Where the murdered embraces the murdered,
Without greeting, and without speech.
You kiss on my neck your mother's heart,
"A brother you may have . . ."[2]
I fling my care on top of your care,
We cry and laugh in two alienations.
Do you ask me how I am?
When you are the answer to that question?
My torment is a jasmine
My death is a kiss without two lips.
I went too far and returned alone,
In me mumbles a grudging old man:

1. *Ya lail ya ain*: the traditional start of popular Arabic song.
2. A proverbial saying of a very close friend.

When? How? Where?
When? How? Where?

Two faces has London: one for Haifa,
And we are companions, rivals and friends.
Love and death record us in the book of land,
An alienation poem of the migrant,
An alienation poem of the homeland.
We reveal our secrets to the domes,
And inscribe our sorrows in the arcades,
And send from our wound nightingale
That rocks the silence of Time.
We knead the massacres bred with our tears.
Do you remember the savory breast
We sucked without appetite?
And an olive tree that left us,
          Like a foreign tourist woman?
And a lover, whose love we did not pity,
But she remained faithful?
Do you remember the days
          We were hungry together,
And when we ate enough together?
When we fell in love together, then we were lost?
Peace be on you. Peace be on me,
On love, born, then dies—Peace be on it,
When it comes back alive!
All singers have grieved mothers,
Every singer has a town,
That sleeps with a star in its heart,
Then wakes up with gangrene in its wound!
We were the sunrise of songs,
Shall we be the sunset of rancor?
From fearful *Ramah* to ancient *Barwah*
To a tear standing between us,

A world rises on the sand, a world falls in the mire,
And our enemies are a curse.
Death recoils, but they creep at ease.
Our supporters . . . false money.
What could I do alone . . . what could you do alone,
When my grave became my cradle
And your cradle your grave?
Shall I sing in your place, and you sing in mine
To an arid, barren desert
Where the singer dies, and is left behind by the caravan?
Shall the mermaid come out of the sea?
From the bottom shells,
Or has the sea covered its secrets?
And we finished, mumbling indignantly:
When? How? Where?

At the shelling hour I wondered:
Was he reached by the shells?
Bowing on the news in the paper?
Was he missed by the shells,
    As he went to have a new drink,
And confide his anguish in a poem?
And I wonder: how is he now
Angry, hungry, cold, frightened?
Was he surprised by the shells?
Was he spared my shells?
On the TV screen I saw your face
In the light of a sunny bomb,
Near you was a baby girl corpse, a jasmine branch,
Mouths agape of love and passion victims. . . .
Ah, horns of my shame and fear
Reverberating in blood, but no one hears or answers
Except the giggles of the Sodom drunk
And the ridicule of Gomorrah and Tel Aviv

I neared my palm to your face, trying to touch it.
On the TV screen, in the light of the sunny bomb
Near you was a baby girl corpse.
On her face was that of my love, Muhammad
And of Waddah, shrieking in fear,
On the TV screen, shrieking in fear,
And pulling at Omar's forearm,
Hoping for a refuge in some pit.
I died. You died. All the humans died;
All the humans! The moon died.
The wind shrouded it secretly,
To bury it in the chaff of trees
Of the world of God and men.
Nothing was left but news, fragments of news.
And near you was a corpse, beside a corpse
And in the heart, a corpse. Nothing near me was
Except my eyes' tears. "One may have a brother. . . ."

Two faces has Paris: one for Haifa,
And we are brothers in dream and folly.
You know my heart, you know my grief,
My love rose, my disappointment.
You see your house in my voice glare
I hear your voice in my house silence.
"One may have a brother. . . ."
I thought of you, because I love my homeland.
You thought of me, because the homeland
—Let alone poetry—does not think of the exiles,
And does not think of the oppressed
—Let alone poetry—how can rock and clay think?
—Let alone poetry—we are the wreckage of songs,
The massacre of wheat and jasmine.
Our children's enemies hit,
Our friends are liars,

And nothing in the Earth is left
Except those who like us dead.
If God decreed good intentions,
They may accept us as refugees,
Weakened, exhausted.
I thought of you, you thought of me,
Because the martyr is a faithful friend.

Two faces has Beirut, one for Haifa,
And we are friends in prison and exile.
Two faces has London, one for Haifa,
We are companions in love and fear.
Two faces has Paris, one for Haifa,
And we are siblings in oppression and tyranny.
Two faces has Tunis, one for Haifa,
We are to strangers, we are to strangers.
We have no Time, we have no Place.
Why? Why? And where, and how?
One face has Haifa.

Ramah, October 27, 1982
(pp. 11–43)

There Is No More Dialogue with You, It Is Simply Another Explosion

It is simply another explosion
You gave up my sorrow burden,
And my life burden,
And laid your death burden on me.
You left the horse alone . . . Why?
You preferred the horizon
As your death horseback,
You preferred my sorrow as refuge,
Answer me, answer me, why?

Our sparrows, my friend, fly without wings,
Our dreams, my companion,
Fly without propeller.
They fly over the water and firetrap,
        And fire and water,
With no place to land on,
        Except the massacre.
They forget their beaks in the earth
        Of the mass graves . . .
Love, love is a forbidden land, my friend,
And the rosary is broken up.
It is fear and death in fear. Security is in death
There is no security in the Security Council,
        My friend!
The Security Council is a neutral land,
Companion!
And we are the torment of roads,
The rancor of directions,
We are the dust of nations,
        The failure of languages,
And some prayer,

On what graves are available.
In death increase the ranks of our casual brothers,
Our casual enemies.
The atmosphere crowds with the affluent,
Who like us dead.
But they like us, my friend,
With all doubts and all certainties.
You emigrated in the sorrow
To the right's falsehood you emigrated,
From falsehood to falsehood
From Babylon to Babylon
To a Babylonian Babylon
From the worthless killer to a worthless ignorant,
From a casual criminal to a surfeited killer,
 From a base liar to a failing imposter
From a transient to a transient,
 To a transient's transient.
And what did you find there except what is not me?
And what did you find there except what is not you?
Brother, let alone this matter,
You love my brother . . . and I love your brother
And you departed. Departed.
And I did not remain alone like the sword.
I am neither a sword nor the wheat stalk.
 And no rose in my right hand, no bomb,
Because I came to the land before you,
I became, with God's will, I became
The first of questions
So, let you be the final of the questions
Perhaps the answers will curtail the problem
And lead to begin with the name of God
To the first light in the mystery tunnel.

You disguised yourself with death.

Our tactics did not obey the strategy
Of waiting for wonders.
There are no armies, no marching, no messing,
No lines, no regiments, no battalions,
No neighborhood, no dialogue, no homes,
No relatives.
You disguised yourself with death,
But the creeping of scorpions
     Was visible to all humans,
Besieging our coffins, companion,
Raiding whereabouts
One after the other.
Of the Bedouins we were, in a dress of jute,
Now we wear a cravat.
Bedouins we were, and so became
Dhubian tribe raids. 'Abs tribe fights.

There they are, my friend, at your door
Zorba's old women, crowding over your torment
Pushing each other: coal and wax.
They sniffed at your death
Before living with death in you.
They searched in my clothes and yours
For the probable wealth, for the secret,
The secret of the poem, the secret of creed,
Its chronic pains
And the secret of your presence,
In your full absence.
They searched for what the will says
Is there a will?
Thickets of smoke and chaff
     Rattling in the death yard.
Where is the will? We want the will
You are neither Xerxes nor Caesar

For you are higher, dearer, and greater
And you are the will,
And the secret of the matter.
But it is the age of ignorance
Yes, my brother in my torment, distress, and exile.
Do you hear me? It is the age of ignorance.
        And nothing in it is much less, except roses
But thorn is more cruel, violent, and more.
Yes, brother, it is the age of ignorance.
None of our band can bear hearing the will,
And you are the will, you are the will,
And God is greater.

You will remember, if God willed you to remember,
And you remember if you wished to remember
That we read Umru'l-Qais under the fear of death
We read together Lorca's sorrow
And the poem in L by Shanfara
Neruda's rancor and Aragon's magic,
Al-Mutanabbi's miracle
Did he not melt Time into a poem
And death into a platform?
We read together Nazim Hikmet's fear
And Ataturk's pining. This real pining
Of our wretched, vagrant brother
Of Muhammad's mother
And the torment baby Muhammad,
The homeland prison for life?
We read together what we wrote together.
        We wrote to our ancient *Barwa*, to our frightened *Ramah*
To Acre, to Haifa, to Amman, to Nezareth,
To Beirut, Damascus, and Cairo,
To the persevering nation,
And the approaching revolution,

And, nothing. Nothing but the charm,
Of our bleeding dreams,
And our motionless clocks,
And the fragments of our revolting pains.
From all your heart you wrote
And you wrote . . . and from my heart
We wrote for a people, with land,
And, for a land, with people.
We wrote with love . . . and for love.
You know we hated pale hatred,
We hated despotic invaders.
     And, no . . . we did not hate the Jews,
     Or the British,
Nor any enemy nation or any friendly nation.
We hated the demons of lying states
Their herds of loose riffraff.
We hated the tracks of a usurping tank,
The wings of the raiding bomber,
And the attack force.
We hated their walls scourge on the neck bones,
Their wedges in the Earth,
     Beyond Earth, beyond the Earth.
They say to the air and land
We try to hurl them into the sea.
They lie!
They laugh a bitter weeping, and implore.
They hurl us to the mirage.
They hurl us to the serpents.
They hurl us to the wolves.
They hurl us to the waste.
They hurl us to the loss of loss.
You know, my friend. You know
That hell is bored with hell,
And it deserted hell.
Why should you die then?

Why should I live then, why?
We die. We live. We die. We die.
For the sarcastic United Nations
And the adultery of its whorish files.
Why? Why? Why? Why? Why?
What is all this destruction, failure, torment,
Why all this? And this? And this?

Remember
And God may rescue a dead man if he remembers,
For God we are. So try then. . . . And remember,
Remember the mother's pleasure
For two mothers in one
And the grace of her *Kubba*, the pride of her table,
The purity of the toasted loaf.
        Remember
A father who is not given to shouting
Or grumbling. . . . Remember
A father who does not fret or complain
About a noisy stay-up till the morning.
Remember much. And do not remember
Much. Some tales are sugar
All myths are distilled poison
And we are the victims of myths,
We are the victims of Nebuchadnezzar,
The orphans of Hitler.
Of our blood red wine is made for the despots;
Of our flesh laurel and rose garlands,
For the invaders are made,
        And musk, and amber.
So do not remember
Fetters and prison and soldiers,
A destroyed house,
A long night, heavy oppression,

And repeated looting.
And do not remember,
    Do not remember, do not remember.

Because we are two friends
In land, people, lifetime, and poetry
We are frank in love and death. . . .
One day I was angry with you . . .
    One day you were angry with me . . .
You had no reason. I had no reason.
Except that we are both of obstinate mettle,
And generous tears.
By day I wrote to you . . . By night you wrote to me.
Our birthday parties have always warned us
Of a hidden secret
A near death . . . a remote dream.
When you celebrated fifty years of life,
The lifetime of the constant wretched,
We laughed together and wept together,
When sang and prayed the rebel friend,
Wishing you a happy birthday
    On oak leaves.
We were born in the morning,
To a dew mother and saffron father,
We died in the evening without parents,
At our sea of exile, in boats of cellophane paper,
On the sea paper. At night
We wrote the drowning song,
Then we turned to burn in the fire
Of the first lines, and the poem burned,
With our tears' fire.
The paper flies with wings of smoke.
And here we are, friend, two pages
With an old face that turns us anew,

On the pages of the anxiety book.
And here we are, not we are,
Dead and alive. Alive and dead.
"My companion wept. . . ."[3]
On the roof of his exile, appealing for help.
"My companion wept. . . ."
He wept. . . . And I wept, on a house roof.
O, I wish, I wish,
And I wish, I wish
That we were born then died on oak leaves.

One day I wrote to you.
     One day you wrote to me:
"I call you a narcissus round my heart."[4]
And your heart is my land,
     And people, and nation.
And your heart . . . is my heart.

They say your death was strange
The strange is that you have lived,
And that I live, and we live. You know,
You know that we were sentenced
A quick death that passes slowly.
You know, you know that we assumed life
By a typographical error.
You know that our execution
Was delayed a thousand times,
As our executioner was drunk,
Over and over.

3. Umru'l-Qais, the earliest pre Islamic Arab poet, addressing his only companion
on his journey to Byzantium, where he died, c. 540 A.D.
   4. A poem by his bosom friend Mahmood.

Glory to God in the highest,
The arrow of speech—peace is on Earth
And for men—except us—pleasure.
Are we among men?
Are we really among men?
Who are we really?
And who are we really?
We asked for the first time,
And for the last time.
The question does not hold,
For the answer to hold.
So, here we are, staying
In one heartbreak after another,
As every alien lives a thousand bewilderments,
And every murder victim carries his grave
On his back.
And probes the galaxy depth . . .
Probes the galaxy depth.

Our mother, Um-Ahmad, embraces me,
In grief, laden with torment of years,
And the burden of longing.
She spreads two frail, scolding palms,
Asking, screaming without voice,
Asking, where is your brother?
Answer, do not hide from me,
Answer, where is Mahmood?
Where is your brother?
Our mother convulses me
With the question.
What should I say to her?
Should I say he went out this morning,
To take his coffee with milk
On the magic pavements

Of the Champs-Elysées?
Or shall I claim you are
        At an urgent meeting?
Shall I claim that you are at a quiet
        Night gathering?
Can I even claim that you have a love tryst,
Meeting a refugee woman writer?
Would she believe that
        You are reciting your poems now
In a hall warmed
By the breath of two thousand
        Of your admirers?
And how should I say, our mother,
That my brother went to see his creator.
My brother, our mother, and met his creator.

⌐

Then you are leaving the home
Of the loved ones.
All right. Now you're leaving
        To the home of the loved ones.
Give them our love:
Rashid Husain, Fadwa Touqan, Tawfiq Zayyad,
Emile Toma, Mu'in Bsaiso, 'Isam Al-'Abbasi,
Yasir Arafat, Emile Habibi, Shaikh Imam,
Ahmad Yasin, Sa'dullah Wannous, Katib Yasin,
George Habash, Najib Mahfooz, Abu-'Ali Mustafa,
Yusuf Hanna, Mamdooh 'Adwan, Khlil Al-Wazir,
Nazih Khair, Raphael Alberti, Naji Al-'Ali,
Isma'il Shammut, Buland Al-Haidari,
        Muhammad Mahdi Al-Jawahiri,
Yanis Ritsos, Alexandre Ben, Yusuf Shahin,
Yusuf Idris, Suhail Idris, Raja' Al-Naqqash,
'Abdulwahhab Al-Bayyati, Ghassan Kanafani,
Nizar Qabbani . . . Enough for me,

Enough for me, many more,
Many more. Give them my love.
In Paradise you shall meet Sami—
Our genuine handsome brother.
Do they play the lute in Paradise?
You love Sami with his lute,
At the `Ain meeting.
Sami departed when he was of your age,
Sixty-seven. No, no I cannot bear that number.
You are eternity, including eternity, deleting eternity.
I know. You shall return.
One new morning you shall return,
To the home, the neighbor, Jerusalem, the sun,
You shall return. Alive you return.
Dead you return. You shall return.
There is no shroud suitable for us,
Except a mother's tear,
        To wet the homeland soil.
And there is no land to suit us, or we suit it,
Except this land.
Homecoming day is near, like doomsday,
The singer's dream is a struggle.
The singer's death is a struggle of the struggle.

So you are departing from the loved ones home,
In a lifeboat, honest sea surface.
I call, companion, your tears.
Where I not holding to a rope from God,
But approaching slowly,
I would have chided you:
Take me with you. Take me with you,
        Take me . . .

Ramah, August 10, 2008
(pp. 67–113)

A Very Personal Conversation
(The Last Day of 2008)

— 059-9262600
— Hello, Mahmood. Answer. Reply. Speak, Mahmood
(Welcome,
The dialed number cannot be reached now,
Please try again later.)

— 059-9262600
— Hammouda. Hello. Answer. Mahmood . . .

(Welcome,
The dialed number cannot be reached now,
Please try again later.)

— 059-9262600
— (Welcome,
The dialed number cannot be reached now,
Please try again later.)

— 059-9262600
Hello, Hello, Hello

(Welcome,
The number dialed cannot be reached now,
Please try again later.)

That is my problem.

That is my grievous dilemma.
How can I live my life as you knew it?
How can I invite you to the family evening party,
On New Year's Eve?
That is my plight, my friend,
And death has its chronic secrets.
My confession is simple and plain:
I miss you, brother.
Dear old boy, I am tired of the arid loneliness.
And I . . . from the top of my cross cry:
My morsel is bitter, brother.
The cups of grief are lethal;
        And I am exhausted with yearning
To a game of backgammon,
In our disappointed evenings,
And our failure days,
Our falling back, refugees to our sorrow
And to being a family, in the useless diaspora.
Exhausted, brother, exhausted.
Memories have burdened my back,
And languages ended in my speech.
My silence has its blizzards,
And massive volcanoes.
My disturbance is severe,
My bewilderment kills me.
In the stations of our flitting appointment,
The trains passed with me, friend,
And I was unaware,
If I was passing or the trains were!
Tired, exhausted.
When should I rest with its mercy,
When shall the caravan take me with it?
Exhausted, exhausted, brother.

— Hello . . .

    (The dialed number cannot be reached now . . .)

Ramah, December 31, 2008

(pp. 115–23)

8

I Regret (2009)

(A Flock Poem)
(Nazareth, Palestine, 2009)

By Way of Introduction . . .
From The Old Testament: Joshua 10:12–28

12- Then spake Joshua to the Lord in the day when the Lord delivered up the Amorites before the children of Israel, and he said in the sight of Israel, Sun, stand thou still upon Gibeon; and thou, moon in the Valley of eye Ajalon. 13- And the sun stood still, and moon stayed, until the people had avenged themselves upon their enemies. Is not this written in the book of Jasher? So the sun stood still in the midst of heaven, and hastened not to go down about a whole day. 14- And there was no day like that before it or after it, that the Lord hearkened unto the voice of a man: for the Lord's fought for Israel. 15- And Joshua returned, and all Israel with him, unto the camp to Gilgal. 16- But these five kings fled, and hid themselves in a cave at Makkedah. 17- And it was told Joshua, saying, the five kings are found hid in a cave at Makkedah. 18- And Joshua said, roll great stones upon the mouth of the cave, and set men by it for to keep them: 19- And stay ye not, but pursue after your enemies and smite the hindmost of them; suffer them not to enter into their cities: for the Lord your God had delivered them into your hand. 20- And it came to pass, when Joshua and the children of Israel had made an end of slaying them with a very great slaughter, till they were consumed, that the rest that remained of them entered into fenced cities. 21- And all the people returned to the camp of Joshua at Makkedah in peace: none moved his tongue against any of the children of Israel. 22- Then said Joshua, open the mouth of the cave, and bring those five kings unto me out of the cave. 23- And they did so, and brought forth those five kings unto him out of the cave, the king of Jerusalem the king of Hebron, the king of Jarmuth, the king of Lachish, and the king of Eglon. 24- And it came to pass, when they brought those kings unto Joshua, that Joshua called for all the men of Israel, and said unto the captains of the men of war who went with him, come near, put your feet upon the necks of these kings. And they came near, and put their feet up on the necks of them. 25- And Joshua said unto them, fear not nor be dismayed, be strong and of good courage: for thus shall the Lord do to all your enemies against whom ye fight. 26- And afterwards Joshua smote them, and slew them, and hanged them on five trees: and they were hanging upon the trees until the evening. 27- And it came to pass at the time of the going down of the sun, that Joshua commanded, and they took them down off the trees, and cast them into the cave wherein they had been hid, and laid great stones in the cave's mouth, which remain until this very day.

My hard life is costly,
Oh, my brother, and rich-poor enemy.
My quick, sudden death is costly.
I regret,
Because I was born outside the system
Of banks and capitals' money markets.
My death stock exchange is my birthplace.
Not to live I was born, but for you to sever my head.
So, I will resist.
Costly, my adversary, is my life.
Costly is my death.
So, I regret.
I do . . . regret.

I ran away from death, was frightened;
And in my death secrets, I hid myself.
To it I took refuge from death.
But, brother, enemy, I died.
Not out of fear I died; I died a death
As you yourself wanted, so I was frightened.
There was no house to protect me,
No illusion to save me, no government
      To do what is Justice.
Therefore, I regret.

You sought to, endeavored, labored so much
To master my murder.
You spent a lot of money
To slaughter me, my children and people,
To slaughter my soil and field trees,
My face, voice, and shadow.
My death prays for me; so tell me
When shall you accept my regret
Because I was born; I swore and still swear
That I regret.

I'll weep and weep, and you sing.
A person called Ocampo
Came by chance from the turning orbit,
Embraced a tank, which became your home,
For dancing the samba, rumba, mambo,
And take from me that which is not yours, Ocampo
And you . . . the weak oppression,
By the strong rule,
Toward what shall I aspire and yearn,
When all that was left
Is fear, sorrow, doubt, and horror?
I weep. You laugh. And Ocampo flaunts.
I weep. You laugh.
Believe me then, my brother and enemy,
Believe me, forgive my life. And pity me.
I do regret.

I was born, as people are born, before and after me.
I dreamt that I will grow up like all humans,
Like birds, and dogs, and trees.
I dreamt. I exceeded my limits.

Briefly, I dreamt, then apologized.
My dream apologized. I do regret.

At your mother's grave,
Under Europe's icy weather, I stopped for long.
I laid my few flowers and plenty of grief.
My pain reminded me of the *Fatihah Surah*.
Your mother's death taught me a lesson,
And taught me the sharp language.
Our night is like the last night.
So what did you learn from your mother's grave,
Tell me, except hating my dream,
And your desire to kill me?
I asked you, look me in the eye,
Master your account, and train your answer,
And tell me:
Why do you formulate
        The arts of tormenting me,
And excel in fighting and humiliating me?
Why do you practice murdering me,
Chopping up my land and people?
Answer me, do not philosophize.
It's time for you to regret,
And pull your heavy shadow
        Off my shadow's back.
        Say you regret.
I do regret.

You know? You have filled my homeland
With mass graves, brother.
        Brother and bold enemy,
Why did you fill my homeland

With mass graves?
Why did you destroy bridges,
Why do you pound down my bones
And build palaces on them?
Why should my home stones
Become walls around your palace?
My homeland is my homeland.
I want it to be the homeland,
With its sweet flourishing gardens,
For us and all the people.
Of my grandfather's skin
You prepare a shroud for my death,
And make a graveyard of my homeland.
I am not grieved or angry or grumbling.
     Here I am, enemy of my life, dying.
In death there is an attitude.
So, I regret. I . . . really regret.

You tell us that God has chosen you.
A guidance for humans,
A light over the dark wretched world,
An atonement for sins.
You swear that you are *über alles*.
But you lie one day,
You steal one day,
You kill one day,
You perjure all the time!
While my wound is purer, higher, cleaner;
My death, nobler.
So can you sympathize, and will you sympathize,
When, my brother, and pious enemy,
Will you regret?

I learned that I am weak,
But no good at weakness;
That I fear, but am no good at fear;
That I am courageous,
But no good at tyranny, oppression, and injustice;
That I am bashful, but no good at violence.
How did you learn, then,
And become what you are?
Where did you come from?
Are you what you are?
Tell me: why do you fight
My origin and lineage?
Why do you try to kill me?
My question is hard. My ignorance is strange.
How would you know what you do not know?
I, brother and meek enemy,
I . . . do regret.

I built a fort, a tower, and a castle, on the sand.
I dispatched a war and Pepsi fleet,
An oil and Cola fleet,
On a tear sea.
I fooled myself that I would defeat
The darkness army, by lighting a candle.
I confess now: my heart is ashes
On torture brands. I built on sand. So demolish!
I built on sand. So explode!
I . . . do regret.

I imagine that your conscience is alive,
And that it warned you
Of my violated pain.
I imagine that your conscious is dead,

And tried to beat you.
But indignation was not saved
By what cannot save.
I will never be like you . . . I do regret.

I'll open my palm to the fortune-teller,
        Unmindful of a secret I was born on.
Unmindful of my death date.
I open my chest and lift my face
To a bomber that you fly,
Oh, my brother and bitter enemy,
So you can spot me and master shell me.
I spread my palm,
As you turn your face round
For fear of a greeting.
You remember my hand is prosthetic;
My old hand remained with you.
And in my shoulder
There remains your splinter.
But you evade, and speak of chance.
You break a promise, forget, and break.
I . . . really regret.

I asked you to try. Try your second birth,
And try your exit of yourself,
To the clear view.
I asked you to learn wisdom of the cruel tear,
To practice my torment a little
To desert your bloody illusions,
And the misery
Of your despotic nightmares
Of the grey ashes in the coffin
Of a bloody holocaust . . .

You will fight me for no use.
You kill me for no use.
I am the surviving wisdom.
I am the cornerstone.
Your wrath is cruel, bloody, and shameful.
My sorrow is honorable.
Do you grieve? Wait. I do regret.
My children will urinate
On the face of your fires.
You are angry? Wait, I do regret.
I shall shine my slippers
With your high banner
I was born to live, live, and live.
Your death sentence on me
Is base and disgusting
I . . . do regret.

Here is the prison,
I know I fell captive,
And know that Joshua the son of Nun
Closed the cave on me,
And heaped around me, above me, under me
The darkness of iron
And the silence of stone.
I realize that Joshua son of Nun
Seeks my death,
        In quiet slowness and all expertise.
I realize that I died as Joshua wanted.
I realize I was resurrected, not as he wanted.
So tell me,
Are you Joshua son of Nun, of Dolly Pedigree?
Now tell me,
Why do you practice capturing and killing me?
Perhaps my question is difficult for you.

Your mind is crying. Your heart is bleeding.
Therefore, I regret.
I . . . do regret.

Your mind is crying. Your heart is bleeding.

I happily reveal my love of life,
The love of beauty,
The love of children.
And you miserably reveal
The love of fighting,
The love of heroism.
Where is gallantry then? Where is manhood?
On a child's body scattered in the braid ashes,
And bone coal, and the remains
Of a murdered mother and sister?
Are those the images of heroism?
But where is heroism?
And how does heroism formulate?
My question is difficult; excuse my few words.
You are short, short. My patient soul is long.
My madness mind raves.
So, I regret. I do regret.

My Ford is little, but not kashrut.
Would you like some tea?
My water is scanty, but not kashrut.
Would you like some tea?
My throat is not right,
My brother and enemy.
I have no biscuits. Would you like some tea?
Sorry, my friend, my enemy, generous in enmity.
I have no tea. I have nothing. You are heavy.
So lighten. I . . . do regret.

You waded in blood and flesh and bones.
You became a demon of rashness and oppression.
You conspired, ventured, gambled,
Shouted at the top of your voice, "Sold!"
You've gained a lot to lose a lot.
     So do not grumble, do not lament.
You will make an effort over effort,
And shout, "Sold!"
And at the end of the race you should lose,
And I will be happy,
And you lose.
I'll open a new wide door,
And you lose;
Announce a feast,
And you lose. I . . . do regret.

Windows of rose and oleander
Overlooking the massacre yard.
Remains of murdered people,
Toys of a slaughtered child
Scattered by the wind, among the piles.
A mirror of the cupboard door
Pierced by the smart bullet.
A dinner table
Where the clean dust hungered
And covered the clean dishes,
Wrapped the spoons and saltshaker.
And a walking stick
Of an old man who crumbled silently.
Limbs of a pregnant woman,
Ruins of a house and a dream,
And you overlook the death scene.

What does the speech iron say?
    And what does the peace rust say?
What does the wind grind with the fan?
    Consider. Suffer. Learn. Speak,
And say you regret.
I . . . do regret.

Your gas bombs extort my tears,
My pulse echoes their rhythm.
My blood wrath defies,
My fire rages. Your snow fires flake.
They pour down and shoot.
So how am I to blame if wrath
Would unsheathe my wrath in your face,
While you raid, steal, erase, efface!
You are short-long,
My patience is long-short.
My grief rises. My death is storming.

One evening, I heard you, one exciting evening,
Singing the love of women.
What kind of women do you love?
Which woman is your escaping gazelle?
Do you proffer her a promising rose?
A giant wheat stalk?
You sing the love of women,
And ask me to sing the love of women.
But you disappoint me.
So how can I sing the love of women
And my sweetheart is a motionless corpse,
Like the steel of your cold knife?
My singing is my weeping.
How can I sing? But I shall sing

I will sing, for my sweetheart, returning
From death, in death, by death.
My only sweetheart,
My returning sweetheart,
From death in your infidel fire.
And I was single by your dying fire,
And I will sing
As you blame my mouth,
And curse my blood prayers, and blaspheme,
Because I sing and stir your grief.
I sing, and my song magic disappoints you
Therefore I regret. I . . . do regret.

You build a house with my house rubble,
Brother, cousin, neighbor,
You mastered the art of building,
You mastered the art of destruction.
So how am I to manage my torment and grief?
And how can you manage your sins,
In the presence of God and men?
How can you manage, my brother,
Cousin, and neighbor?
How can you say "raiding my fence,"
And how can you say "my siege,"
Yet you will hush my protesting voice,
My brother, cousin, and neighbor?
How can you say: I regret? I . . . do regret.

Suppose I am a swallow,
Taking refuge in an old ceiling,
Crumbling, under shelling;
Tell me, why do you destroy my nest dreams?

My chance to live,
So my dream becomes my coffin. Why?
Suppose my house is nothing but an anthill,
Courting a wheat grain
Why do the belts of the death tank
Crush my house,
And the terror bomber
Pound my wheat grain and my voice?
Is Abyssinian Abraha your father?[1]
Then who could Avraham be?
What is Hagar's sin,
    So you burden her with hell weight?
I am Hagar's child.
    I know I have grown up a little,
And that you are worried about my growth.
Hagar, my old mother, nursed me.
Then I grow up a little on wretched Hagar's milk.
No, I did not steal your milk.
Your mother is not my mother;
Your milk is not my milk.
Why do you charge?
How do you attack and thunder,
And your soul's phosphorus sparks with shame?
Your flames consume my soul's walls.
Why?
Qais and Layla have a beautiful love story.
Romeo and Juliet have a long love tale.
What can you say to Lu'ay's eyes and Jamila's legs?
Do you know how to say "I regret!" Do you?

---

1. Abraha, the Abyssinian army general, who came to Yemen representing the Byzantine empire, to control parts of the country and destroy Ka`ba and control the Arabs. Died c. 555 A.D.

Because I am your brother in the Holocaust,
I bore your torment over mine.
All victims are relatives.
I told people's lands; all peoples, all lands.
Grieved and angry,
At the thickening darkness of the horizons.
And you destroy the seaweed sorrow,
And shell the love mint by air, and land and sea,
And stick your paws in the balcony's joy.
        Why do you sever the braids,
To braid gallows for hanging childhood necks,
And gouge dreamy eyes with scanty light,
Roving the scanty sky?
Do you defeat an eye you gouged,
A leg you amputated,
        Defeat a heart you crashed,
A head you severed?
Do you defeat? No, you are defeated.
You wither and age.
You degenerate and fall. God wins!
The winner is God!
Say you regret. I . . . do regret.

Details retreat their steps for consideration.
The gravity apple goes up by the force,
To its branch.
Snows return to water
In the primordial form.
Clouds return to water. Soil restores its power
Of zodiacal air to the fire.
The steppes people were vegetarian.
Hunger joined the fang, the claw to the flesh.

But cannibalism is different;
An antique time that passed.
The book of madness was burned,
And the age of insomnia,
And the age of regret.
Man of this later time
Restores the shine to it.
So say you regret
About all this madness,
Degeneration, and drowning.
I regret. I . . . do regret.

Your house garden is carefully planned.
Your furniture is superb.
There are oil paintings, black and white,
    And water color
Decorating the walls of your grand salon.
All right! Here you are listening deeply,
Sedately, gravely to the tunes of Mozart,
And of the deaf genius, Beethoven;
To the poems of Shakespeare,
Goethe, Byron, and Lorca.
    On the balconies of your shelves
Are some novels by Marquez,
Ibsen, Gorky, Pushkin,
Mahfouz is also there.
You chew lettuce and ask for a drink.
Your exquisite computer mouse
Opens Google horizons
And a new door.
You go deep and open a new wound
In my heart door. You go deep,
And open my people's artery.
You go deep and you block my way. Why?

You strike East by West. Why?
You like the book, but after reading
You assassinate the author's heart,
The author's soul. Say you regret!
Yes, regret. I . . . do regret.

Your children are all around me.
They pace by my house,
        Bedroom, and field.
I caress their chaotic blonde hair,
And feed them my homemade bread
And family cake.
Why do you caress my child
With fire and gas?
Why do you pour lead on me
And erase from your soul shadows
        My soul and shadow.
Why?
Answer me. Why do you mince your words,
Soft, sweet, and pleasant,
While your deed is disgusting
        And so nauseating?
I see you and hear what you say
And not say. So, I regret.
Times have passed your hands,
Seasons have passed you over.
Origins are dead for you.
So, I regret. I . . . do regret.

Do you remember? A thousand years ago,
You lost directions? The compass was lost
In your horizon. You walked, asked, pleaded.
The ignoring nations were unable

To put up with you.
When you were tired, you found rest
    In my home lap.
Hungry, you lived on some of my fruits.
A cover for your nakedness was my dress.
Your bread was my wheat, water, and fire.
I did not need your thanks,
You were my brother in heaven. On Earth,
    You were my companion and neighbor.
Our prophet advised to support,
And help the seventh neighbor.
I did not ask for thanks.
God has a stand. People have a stand.
You know, but you deviate.
So, I regret. Yes, I regret. I . . . do regret.

More thorns and brands, oh, master
    Of snow and fire. Heap more thorns,
    And brands, and make my path difficult
    And formidable. I walked on water for long,
My miracle is still at the start.
I walked, treading on water,
So let me walk, treading on thorns
    And brands. My miracle is nearing the end.
Who are you to question my miracle
In life, with a circus game,
And a jump on a short, short rope!
And who are you to block the way
On what destiny wills
And what destiny will be!
You were ignorant of so much,
And waded in more ignorance,
To know what you do not know.
Therefore, I regret.

I am and all nations are in winter,
You are in summer.
Yes, I regret. I . . . do regret.

I spell out the clarity of your ambiguity
In a frank, frank speech.
From Jerusalem was Jericho,
Gazza was from Jerusalem.
You may kill someone murdered,
And wound a wounded.
On the Nations Organization
You relied for long.
At the Security Council
You enjoyed your food
And dessert plates,
And Coke, Pepsi, Cola,
And a happy, comfortable sleep.
Your way is to provoke, exceed, and violate,
To wear death, an ugly face and ugly heart.
I say frankly, frankly,
I tell you now you are tired and exhausted.
You have violated every tradition,
And eluded every law.
But you will never have peace
Because the fans are tied to the winds.
The weather secret is profound.
And one wind changes another.
One wind reproaches another.
One and punishes another.
And you will have no rest
Because Hell is singing and Gehenna fire tunes
So I regret. I . . . do regret.

Clothes racks have a weight limit,
Waves and fire have their limits,
A limit for what you and I can take.
I try a light cascade.
You create a blood cascade.
I make shoes for a child to walk,
You make shoes for a child
     To break his feet.
You wade in illusion,
You wade towards extinction,
Your footsteps are lost,
     Your footsteps' echo is lost.
Before the ancient antiquity,
You slaughtered, spilled, and from the skin
Of my grandfathers' grandfathers,
You hoisted the banner
On a corpse that never slept
But stays up, stays up in the fair of pain,
With a never-tiring praise,
And an ever-active chant.
And intoning that never obeys,
     And a pious call that is never lost.
Perhaps the hurricanes will come
To carry me from my death cellars
And set free my voice
To raise my call for prayer
And the bells of my grief,
Over all and every top,
For the whole nations to view
That you are cruel,
Cruel, rude, crude and unjust.
Therefore I regret. So I regret.
I . . . do regret.

Blessed be the sun, the wind,
The mountain narcissus.
     Blessed be the passion of songs,
Rite after rite, a wedding after a wedding.
Blessed be the new miracles.
My mother is blessed among women.
Blessed be my father's face,
My father's heart.
His hands are blessed.
My offering desires, and Earth offers
What the sky responds.
Blessed be the prayer in you.
O, Lord, bless my steps.
O, Lord, forgive my sins and pardon my guilt.
I accepted your glory, an ultimate and only Lord,
Accept my prayers. Steady my stumbles.
Answer me. Relieve me,
Punish my despotic, violent invaders.
Lord, bless my olive's meekness
And my lemon's prayers.
Lord, bless my resort to you
Away from oppression, subjugation, and evil.
Lord, protect me and increase your guidance,
Guide my brother-enemy
To hear my grief, and see my voice.
My brother-enemy,
I have planted a wheat stalk for life
A lily for all parts
But you are spreading havoc and destruction
So regret. Yes, regret.
And yes, regret. I . . . do regret.

You learned to play the piano, when young;
You mastered the works of Bach,

And those of Schubert and Chopin.
But you argued with Wagner.
Why do you believe
What was randomly said of him,
And spend your youth in playing the gun,
And avenging your sister?
What have I to do with Wagner,
That you take revenge on him and me?
Answer me!
Why did you learn playing with bullets,
And you still play music?
You ask me for salvation,
And I ask for my salvation from you.
Why did you learn tuning with bullets
And you still play music?
My brother-enemy, I regret.
Yes, I regret. I . . . do regret.

You boast before the nations
That the sky has chosen you
As the messenger of civilization;
That you are the light of nations;
That you are worthy, your people
Are the source of worth.
You flaunt, and raise a sword
Before the nations,
And raise a sword on me.
And hurl me into the cave
Of my despair and death.
And block the cave entrance,
With iron malice and stone deceit.
You dance in my death wedding.
You stone my house and explode.
You bridle my dream,

And weep, and shell,
Complain and storm,
Raid, exceed and explode.
So what can you say?
How do you philosophize?
And what, where, why, how?
What, what is all this? What?
What?

      I regret, yes . . . regret. I . . . do regret.

You played for long.
You played with the fires
Of heavens and earth.
You hid a hybrid secret,
Which was lately revealed.
People cannot accept injustice from people.
Their morals are civilization physics.
A right, declared day and night.
A sand clock.
This long corridor before you,
The marble hall is poorly lit.
The frames' silence is bleeding ink.
Do you write poetry?
Please, let your brother listen to some poetry.
Our time is over, my friend-enemy;
Some poetry may help a little.
Do you realize, we have much grown old.
There is no corridor to lead to early sun.
The marble hall is frightful,
The frames' snow is cruel.
Why do we, then, my brother-enemy
Venture with time?
Age is a shadow. Life fever is a mirage.
So let us live it up, at ease,

My mortal friend
Consider, consider a little, suffer a little,
Learn a little the life climate
So normal, clean, and honorable.
     And say you regret. I . . . do regret.

Finally, before the last one, you returned
From a month-long war, and an age short,
On Lebanon's land.
Alive, but grieved, returned,
And here you are, alive,
     Peeling an apple
Under a beach parasol,
Lying in the sand bed
In your loose swimming suit.
Near you is a cold beer bottle
(I see you prefer Heineken beer!)
And a sweet promising girlfriend.
You returned from the war
(After you hit a mine)
That is your lot.
The mine, my friend-enemy, can hit you.
And this is your lot.
You return alive but . . . on your one leg.
And here you are, after absence and torture,
Returned to a pleasant life,
And the warm and soft beach,
And cold beer.
(You like Heineken then!)
And you still dream of war.
Tell me, why do they dream of war?
Tell me, what is the use?
Perhaps you mistake,
When you live on war, by war, in war,

And for war, and for the strong fist.
Accept my death advice
And the sermon of still corpses
And their dying fires,
Then try, and say you regret.
I . . . do regret.

⸺

Your silk, this exciting obscurity,
Goes back to the cocoon eternity,
Your face dictates on a lily
Its disturbing wrinkles.
I ask. I ask. I ask:
Were you alone at the Holocaust?
Was I not with you,
Lulling my heart and yours
With what the exhausted language can say?
So be just, my friend,
And be wise, my enemy,
Be fair and say you regret.
I do regret.

⸺

For you I pour bittersweet Arabian coffee
With cardamom.
For you I pour tea with mint
From my plantation,
And if you wish, Cola and Pepsi.
Good hospitality is my way.
Have some tamarind drink,
Have some of my citrus blossom water.
I pour; and you pour bullets
And rancor rains
On me. So I regret.
I answer and will keep on

Answering; will count, answer
And will repel, with my palms
And eye spear and heart,
With my people's crosses.
And in the rocks I open my way,
And in the mud and thorn and firebrands,
I will widen a road for my road,
And shout, and shout until I am answered,
By the volcanoes' roar from every side,
And strike, and strike a horror with horror,
Until you realize that I have sworn
By my land and home and Lord,
It is time for you to open your eyes to see me,
And feel ashamed of what I suffer
And swear. I . . . do regret.

A drizzle I am, in the wide space, a drizzle.
My lifetime is that of a drizzle.
My memory is the Oaf and Mejana song,[2]
And a bomber that shelled our quarters;
A girl that flew away, with the wind, and night.
She flew far away.
I search for her, and weep on her.
But there is neither here nor there.
My grief is a drizzle, patting childhood hair;
A moon I have within me,
Weeping for my extinction,
And I cry for its eclipse.
I have a chant among the chants,
Which has become a homeland.
Between the limit and the other limit,

2. Two types of popular songs.

There is the horizon of my impossible tale.
In the center of my soul
There is another, with my soul.
I am my death and resurrection,
And my miracle in the drizzle
Of heavens and earth
Floating, and offering its loved ones
Its freshness to drink.
     Drizzle I am,
So, my brother-enemy, be a drizzle,
And be a drop for thirsty wheat stalks
Be a possible good fruit,
And be the shiver of a rose with fragrance.
Be paper for writing,
Be a lily,
And lives a disbeliever-believer
To die a believer-disbeliever
And say to life . . . say to creation,
Say to nature, say to the being,
Drizzle am I.
And say I am sorry
For what I have done
And what is done
Of you, of me.
I regret. I . . . do regret.

I held together around my horrible,
Secret explosions.
I gathered my fractions in the lute tune
Oh night, Oh eye.[3]
The wedding party did not hide my cares

3. *Yalail, Ya`in* (O, Night . . . O, Eye): the traditional opening of a song.

Nor did the traffic accident disrupt my tango,
To restore to me my exciting youth.
But I do not hide my admission
That I withdrew a little.
The impact on my foot,
From hitting the ground, is obvious.
I withdrew from the youthful
Northern *dabka* dance.
I suffered from a foot fractured,
By the moods of Time,
On the main street,
Between my grief and my grief.
I know that I will remain
The singing singer
The roaring pleading is my voice.
The creation ear is my ear
The singing glory blesses
My terrible aspiration,
To a peak, with no human, or jinni.
From there I sing to it,
To my home window, my gravestone,
And prison bars,
And here between me and me,
The yearning of simple life throughout life,
Around countries and across nations,
And here between me and me,
The despot's last desire,
The invader's last whisper,
The confession voice, of the enemy of life.
I regret. I do regret.

The shelling dust settled respectfully
On the surface of my hot coffee.
When the thick dust rested,

I had the courage to drink the hot coffee.
Alas, for my coffee.
And this sweet and charming hour.
Because I turned away. It remained there
In its cup, annoyed with the clatter of shells.
I do not drink the coffee cold,
With the uproar of bombers,
And under the shells' dust.
I drink it in a new morning,
When grief has shot down a returning bomber
With its insipid insolent game.
I'll have my hot coffee
With flowers around me, and no dust.
Any roses for the flower vase?
You have pounded my bones,
From which I molded the vase.
I decorated it with my sketches:
Here is a nightingale. A gazelle is there.
Two bewitching eyes, dazzled,
Guarding a beautiful heart door.
You pounded my bones.
From them I made flowers
Similar to Galilee flowers,
Suggesting Gaza lemons,
Similar to the olives of Jerusalem,
And mountainous Ramah,
Like Jericho bananas,
And a vineyard in Hebron.
You pounded my bones.
And from them I molded the vase,
But are there no roses for the vase?
That is not fair!
I want roses to suit my bones' grief,
And look like the peace dream.
But you are behind me,

(Like Tariq's speech)[4]
And you are before me.
But there is no supporter, no consoler,
No Security Council,
No one to steady a stumble, no succor.
     I regret. I . . . do regret.

Restore to the swings the childhood horizon.
Feed the garden pigeons. Water the flowers.
Do not suffocate the innocent laughter.
Restore my imagination to me,
My innocent imagination,
My dream of ripe happiness fruits.
Your brother I am, O, my mortal enemy,
Your brother, so do not cut me short
By your reckless slogans.
I carried my soul butterfly to you,
So keep your hawks away from me.
And stop your boisterous hurricanes
At the seaside, my sea.
In a fishing boat I catch my daily
And family living,
But you catch me by the gunboat.
Why? Why? Answer me,
In your clear language
Or in your common speech.
You find me whatever mistake you like.
Have I made a mistake?
If one day I have, or a one day did wrong,
Then pound on my door with your soul fist,

4. Tariq bin Ziad, conqueror of Andalus in 711, addressing his forces: "The sea is behind, the enemy is before you."

And question, argue with my answer,
Debate with my torture,
Refute my argument,
To hear from me: I regret.
You did a lot of wrong,
Made more mistakes.
So do not turn a tiger, or a despot
And say you regret. I . . . do regret.

Let the sea roar as it pleases.
Let the wind chant the way it claims.
Let roses grow and never stop.
Let the grass rise.
Let to nature its own ways.
Oh, brother and dear enemy,
How can you blame the game,
If it did not bless the skill of the hunter?
And tell me,
Why do you want the wound of the wounded
To fall in love with your weapon?
Then ask my corpse to die in love
With its executioner?
And you want I should look for shadow
        Under your wing,
As my heart weeps and laughs,
And you punish my mother
        For loving her children?
I resort to the Lord of peace
And you resort to the Lord of weapons.
You wake up the Lord of hosts,
The Lord of barricades and bombers!
The phosphorus of your light
        Dims and blinds.
Your light darkness betrays

Your hidden secret,
Oh, my friend and mortal enemy.
You crossed the borders,
You passed every frontier,
Will you return with a shred of light?
When are you coming back,
With a bouquet of flowers?
Will you come back?
Are you returning?
The war disturbs you very much.
The war disturbs you indeed.
So you ask what happened to the dogs,
What will happen to the cats.
And to save them you draw plans on plans.
But, pardon me,
Do you pay attention to a murdered child
That fell to collect his remains
In the heap of rubble,
And what ran of his blood
And mixed with the soil?
Perhaps my question is not reasonable;
But, my brother and reasonable enemy,
It is only a question.
        Only a small question.
Did this question annoy you?
I regret. I . . . do regret.

The hookah headache is the unemployment business.
We know that collusion food is bitter.
Has the noon bus passed?
Say, did you see the thin boy selling copper,
And displaying his mastic chewing gum on the street
Offering candles to the noon sun?
Be careful. The oak does not remember

The eucalyptus adolescence.
The body cannot accept a foreign member
If it does not suit its cells.
Wait. Please smoke if you wish.
You have polluted our atmosphere
A long time ago. No problem.
My patience is long, as much as I can keep it.
My lifetime is short, as much as you will.
Your glass has rebuffed my bullets.
You waded your fill in wrong doings.
You turned my pious olive tree to an infidel.
Your tongue spear is deep in its living blood.
Enough! Do not exaggerate
My evidence against you is strong and decisive.
It is time for you to retract from your night error.
It is time for the morning rise,
For you to see a simple utterance,
Honestly saying, I regret. I do regret.
It is the lesson of creation.
Carpets of grass and roses,
An old book. Spectacles exhausted by reading.
Whence do the honored guests come,
While all your ways are guarded
By watchdogs? Take a break to consider,
Here is a slate, with Ten Commandments,
One lord and a calf.
Here are twenty slates, and no commandments.
Here is a wide land, and people who desire life,
And new healthy offspring, free and fair.
There are no pharaohs outside the rocks,
And poetry and archaeology.
Wait for the express mail, your nervous e-mail.
Wait for a fresh rose and a wonderful song
About the returnees to the lost moment.
Stop the madness rage!

Stop iron nonsense!
Stop my nightmares and yours!
Stop, and say I regret. I . . . do regret.

⸻

You live. And how can you live
On an illusion's illusion?
Did God choose you as one unique nation?
Please, be introduced to God's poets.
Choose your path: towards light, wheat, and love.
Or, please, towards where you are,
A darkness hostage, a prisoner
To your futile myths,
And choose for your children a new horizon
Of jasmine. From the human joy wheat
Learn to read your soul among my book lines.
Converse with my torment.
A prisoner of your mirrors you are,
Drowned in fog.
Your sand clock is assassinated by Time.
So, come out to the sun and people.
Do not turn backwards.
Leave your darkness with no return.
Your ambition is remote from the land,
And from what life wants
Remote! From its desires you are in arrears.
So, say to the Time. Say to the Place,
      And say to me,
Say to life, I regret. I . . . do regret.

⸻

Here is the bleeding of my wounds
Listen a bit, to hear from me my spirit psalms.
I am not David. David is one, Samih another.
My torment is a prayer echoing Jesus' torment.

My mother's grief recalls those of Jesus' mother's,
And similar to me is what the psalms say
From ancient times.
Similar to me is what I say
But your speech is strange.
By the light of your spirit's phosphorus,
In the soul's darkness,
You broke away, distanced yourself, left,
Departed from your soul light.
So listen to my soul psalms, very clearly,
A speech purified by fire, grief, and oil,
Wounded revelation, a far-aspiring dream.
My death suggests your death.
My healthy, pure resentment cries:
Suffice my torment. Enough for me Christ's cross.
When will you rest from war and shelling,
So I can rest.
I bled a lot. I bled for long.
    I am still bleeding.
So say you regret. I . . . do regret.

    The marriage of wheat stalks and fire
    Is a futile rite.
For zinc, water, and roses
Are born children of a spiteful mine,
Contrary to other walkers' dreams.
From firebrands, wheat, almonds, and cotton
An oil barrel is born.
From a perfume vial is born
An oil barrel and a cartridge clip,
An idea is born
To roam the galaxy. In every town
The evening repeats to me
The perennial question, "Whence do we begin?"

The morning star gives her answer
By asking, "Whither shall we go?"
A comet falls and asks,
"Where are the sky limits?
And Earth, where are your limits?"
Surprising came these questions.
The problem begins,
My heart pounds. Life-fever beats
The drums of the old-new struggle.
From nowhere comes a voice,
      Piercing the darkness:
A day for evil, an age for good.
The ashes' heart pounds
With its future Phoenix.
I lift my old-new face
To the amazing prayer direction;
To God I lift a despair face
And distraction hands.
I was for Him what he wants.
I am still for Him.
I lift my face from Golgotha.
I lift my soul a veil to my face,
And lift my face . . .
To God, I lift my eyes.
      I raise my heart and hands.
Oh, Lord, grief I grieved,
Orphanhood exhausted me,
Fire destroyed my field and food.
Weeping, I wept and turned my face
To your throne light.
Oh, Lord, nations wronged me,
Roads were blocked before me,
I implored, prayed, my voice turned hoarse,
My water springs fell short,
My calls continued, I lighted my candles,

Excuse my weeping and wipe off my tears.
My darkness is thick,
My night is long and heavy.
Grace me with Heaven's light,
Renew my glow, and guide my steps
To cross my exile.
Oh, Lord, forgive my sins, accept my plea,
I suffered misery, my clothes wore out,
Depression cold is cruel,
Surrender heat is hateful.
I suffered misery.
The military chased me,
Away from my house door.
I plead with my life for death.
My fire flares with my oil.
My silence rocks my silence,
And pulls down my top.
No top is left but Yours,
No voice but Yours.
Oh, Lord, bless my spirit volcanoes.
Relieve my wounds,
Glorify with your Time
What is left of my little time.
My God, there is no god but You.
My pastures are laden
With vicious, poisonous weeds.
My sheep expired on my hands
They heaped the rocks into my well.
I have a fig tree that they spoiled,
An olive tree that they scraped;
I have a palm tree that they scolded,
A vineyard that they rebuked,
A lemon tree that they chopped,
A mint plant that they dried
As a punishment.

So how can I exude my grief and weakness,
And how can it reveal my fear, for it and me.
My God, there is no god but You.
I see You with my heart and soul.
I see You; You see me a prisoner of snares.
My father's land became a graveyard.
The homes of believers became a waste.
The orchards of believers became a desert.
Their schools are denied.
Their sorrows are rainy darkness.
My God, there is no god but You.
I asked Your forgiveness,
I sought Your forgiveness.
I implored, prayed, offer me Your forgiveness.
Set on the bombers, set on the missiles
Complete destruction.
And send to us the angel wing.
My God, my God, is there forgiveness?
Is there forgiveness?
And no forgiveness, my God?
My torment is long, cruel, and regrettable.
And You are forgiving, merciful, and fair.
My God, my God, I regret.
I . . . do regret. I . . . do regret.

Ramah, Palestine, January 21, 2009
(pp. 7–114)

— 9 —

Collage 2 (2009)

Selections
[Haifa, Palestine, 2009]

Your eyes are enchanting. I know.
Your swaying stature is a lily, a wheat stalk,
I know. Your cheeks are young and ripe.
Replete, with astounding fragrance.
Ah, my desire star,
Your delicate diminutive mouth,
I know. Your elegant fingers
Are the charm of lemon and oleander.
Ah, I know. Shall I greet you
With my palms offered health and bliss
By your palms?
You are the very beauty, you.
I heard, and obeyed,
But my eyes did not obey.
Ah, my passion, oh, my sorrow,
I was born, since I was born, blind!

(p. 17)

The creature rises from among the worlds.
Really, the creature was.
Really. I see him with what saves
The light of faith in the name of God, and man.
I see among my fingers the faces of things,
And see states, newspapers, satellite,
The shadow of forms and the rainbow,
And see freedom prisoners,
In the dark dungeons.
I see the features of the prison warden;
Between my fingers I see armies and battlefields.
I see conferences.
I see rivers, trees, and birds,

Fluttering, among the branches.
Between my toes I see plains, mountains,
Horses and lions, galloping to hunt gazelles.
I see barracks and music institutes.
I see forums of absent reason.
I see sessions of false poetry,
And dinosaurs from antique times,
Under the rubble of times.
Between my fingers I see my toes,
And between my toes I see my fingers,
And die in peace and clear conscience.
Really. The creature was,
Really he was.

(p. 31)

There is nothing but God's light, and God's shadow
On the face of the word.
The word
Is dreams, nations and tribes,
Children, roads, beacons,
Flowers and homes.
The word, nothing but the word
Is man's lethal poison,
The mass destruction weapon.
The word
Is death, and life.
The word
Is God's Soul, God's face, God's light.
Nothing but it. Nothing but Him.

(p. 33)

They pass across the Earth,
Blind and deaf.

No soil. No speech. No fruit.
They are forgotten for an age.
Sometimes they are counted,
Counted among men,
Then they leave, as a strange dim shadow,
With no trace.

(p. 54)

Banners and platoons,
Battalions and armies,
Subdivisions, divisions, and tribes,
Traps and catastrophes.
It did not return from its long absence,
Our master, the absent reason.

(pp. 54–55)

An active dancer, with heavy buttocks,
And huge shoes,
Turning around the bald man
With the dark glasses and two potbellies,
Hoping he will offer her a few pennies.
She turns in her eastern dance,
With her vulgar coquettish vibrations,
Unaware that the one sunk
In his leather settee,
Under the smoke of the nightclub,
Has died, having swallowed but two drinks.
He died at her dance, by heart attack.

(p. 61)

I am the last one, sitting at this table,
Arguing . . . but for no use.

I try to sort out my recurring sorrows,
And know that there is no use.
I am the last of the extinct Arabs.

(p. 63)

O, you falsified!
You, inhabitants of Arab lands.
It is time you lifted your heavy hands
Off the Arab minority,
Oppressed and subdued,
Living among you,
In the figurative countries.

(p. 66)

I return home from work.
My children's mother
Returns from the work worry
To the kitchen worry:
What shall we eat?
She hurries to the ready food in the fridge,
Asking the help of the microwave.
I sacrifice my soul for my children's mother,
But I detest microwave food.
May God help me!
And help you, my children's mother;
And help the microwave!

(pp. 81–82)

Their maps, a book on the Levant,
From tourism companies,
Some canned food and wine,
A pouch on the back,

A hat, and a camera. They fall on me.
Touring what is left of my homeland,
And what is left, if anything,
Of my homeland.
They speak all languages. Here is Babylon.
A Babylon of language roar.
I keep silent, a tower on the seaside,
A tower, whose rocks come
    From Galilee Mountains.
    Its eyes are windows opening on Jerusalem,
Windows on never-ending deserts.
My shadow withdrew beyond the suns.
    Withdrew, withdrew, withdrew.

(pp. 96–97)

I confess, I am an optimist.
In the thorn, I see a flower.
And in my shroud I see an evening dress.
In my victims I see armies and tribes.
An optimist.
O, my soul, my despair,
An optimist.

(p. 111)

Do not fall into her traps.
Do not believe. In her fragrance,
A righteous bee committed suicide.
This vicious rose was born a rose.
But her mother is a salty soil.
Do not fall into her traps.

(p. 135)

I was a captive in the prison
Of exile, loneliness, and wind.
As a punishment, the Israeli army
Made me work at the morgue ward,
At a Rumpam hospital.
I made friends with the dead,
With doctors, on duty.
For the whole of my brief lifetime,
I remember a whisper by a corpse.
"Give my love to my family,
Do not forget, Samih."
Throughout my brief lifetime,
I'm chased by my bitter anger:
I could not find the corpse's family.

(p. 141)

I say to you, Doomsday is imminent
Because the ugly wars are now called
Beautiful piece!
The peace crow
Is now a pigeon.
I say to you, Doomsday is not imminent,
Because the invaders' madness
And the oppressors' ugliness
Is a cloud.
Then, Doomsday is near
Doomsday is near.

(pp. 146–47)

The grass was asked:
"Who are you?"
It said: Quietude.
It was asked, "Who could you be, wind?"

It answered: I am called a refuge.
The sea was asked, "Who are you?"
It replied: Absurdity.
The volcano said: I am called the incident.
The stars replied: My name is ablution.
Darkness replied, I am called corpses.
We asked the mountain:
"Who could you be?"
It replied: Boredom.
We asked the song:
"Who could you be?"
The stillness answered for it,
Coming from a distance:
Hope!

(p. 157)

I do not like you, death!
But I do not fear you!
You are too small for me.
Your shores are too narrow for my sea.
You drown in me, death.
You shall drown in me, death,
And will die yearning for me.
Your bed is my body,
My soul is your quilt.
Please, come in, I do not fear you.
I do not fear you.

(January 20, 2004)
(pp. 158–59)

~ *10* ~

Regardless (2012)

Selections
[Haifa, Palestine, 2012]

In the Beginning Was Ariha

(Our Cana`anite Palestinian Arabian town is ten thousand years old.
It is Yerihu-Ariha, the first town in the world).

The laden heart calls your heart,
You, early dream.
So open your silence windows,
And listen to your lover's call,
You, early dream.
From our old-new stone age
My heart has been calling your heart.
Oh, early dream.
Count on the palm fronds of ten thousand years,
Paving my way and yours
With purity of martyrdom, dates, and memories,
Rising from heavy darkness
On the migration of early Arabs
On desert wings and lofty banners
To the blood-red tear of joy
And a vision training my people and yours
To reveal, until they proclaim:
Here is the cornerstone,
Here is the beginning.
In the beginning was Ariha,
And in the beginning remains Ariha.

I am Canaan's son, of Ya`rub pedigree.
I spoke out the island in poetry,
And formulated Arabism in a language
Of palm trees and roses.

I moved northwards to pastures
Around peaceful waters
In the manner God planned
For His dreaming creatures
And restive cavaliers.
My steeds' hoofs tattooed the rock of Time.
I spread my soul and body
On the universe, as soul and body.
I fought evil, resisted oppression,
Created a world within the world,
And blessed a faith, by a faith,
And singing one day after another,
Witnessing a soul, after another.
Here is the beginning.
In the beginning was Ariha
And will remain Ariha.

I planted my palm trees, house, roses, and offspring.
I perfumed my bananas
With the breath of my old grandfather.
I chanted to the wheat the chance of river
And rich cloud.
I prayed at the star temple
For the immaculate power,
By the solemn revelation magic
        And impressive verses.
I fell prostrate for the great Lord of Existence
I calmed the volcano wrath
        And groomed the rock,
Tamed a river and a wind.
I declared, in the name of heaven and soil,
My fire teachings and my path light,
The straight path of my blood.
The early news of my dream,

My restive advice: Here is the beginning.
In the beginning was Ariha,
And will remain Ariha.

Who is that fellow? Who is that sudden intruder?
Who is that raider on mad horseback?
Raising a wicked villainous sword,
Shedding darkness and death,
Halting the sun to destroy field and food?
Who is this who wages a treacherous war,
Dreaming to settle. I swear he will not settle.
        Rahab's trick is gone.
Misery will not beget another Rahab,
Joshua ben Nun is a smoke image and dust shadow
Who passed by the riverbank.
Joshua ben Nun comes and leaves,
And comes and leaves.
Joshua ben Nun leaves and leaves,
And will not settle, will not settle, will not settle.
The new Ariha wall is my ribs and neck vein
Hidden, visible, strong Ariha wall
Is impregnable against invaders.
Joshua ben Nun will not settle
Joshua ben Nun is the ruins of memory,
On which I cooked my torment . . .
        Olibanum and myrrh
And returned fair, alive, and free
Singing: Here is the beginning.
In the beginning was Ariha,
And remains Ariha,
Remains, remains, remains Ariha.
Here is the beginning,
In the accent of grandfather Canaan,
It was Yerihu,

A refuge for moonlight,
A happy dream in the tree's shade,
And Canaan resting in its hall.
Yerihu was as Jebus desired to be
The bright fair face of life,
The heart of austere struggle.
Yerihu said,
A poet from my land will fall in love with me,
And sing me unlike what all men sang before.
So reveal the aged passion,
A divine wine, allowed by heavens,
And you are in love with Yerihu.
Your fire is the Song of Songs,
Your soul's wheat, the song's heart.
So speak out her love, Samih,
And sing for her, Samih,
And sing, following the rule of God and love,
Yerihu's glory.
It is the war. In the accent of grandfather Ya`rub,
Pronounce it Ariha
Here is the beginning.
        In the beginning was Yerihu,
In the beginning was Ariha.
Remains forever. Remains Ariha.
And remains, remains, Ariha.

It is the war.
From Ben Nun's sword
Is born Nebuchadnezzar.
And born is Xerxes' club
And Caesar's dagger.
From the invasion dagger
Are born a thousand daggers.
All right.

Ariha's patience is wholesome.
        My heart is large.
All right.
Little invaders come.
        Big invaders come.
All right. All right. God is greater.
Ben Nun is smaller,
And smaller is Nebuchadnezzar,
Xerxes and Caesar
And Zion is smaller
For us is love and God. And God is greater.
God is greater. God is greater.

Peek on me Ariha. . . . Peek,
For you I prayed for a thousand years,
So, pray for me.
Don't you remember?
Yes, you do remember. I came to you of late,
A dream cloud, and dates and roses,
Sprinkling a cloud
On Companions' prayers.
I came to you at the height of the message
As God was raising His Book,
        On my spear.
I came, named Khalid.
God blessed my soul as a sword
I came to you, named Hisham,
Trailing the robes,
Filling the hearts, spreading marble.
Do not underestimate this rubble.
In your name my new palace will rise,
And I shall call you my happy feast,
And will blow off the dust from your lips.
And wipe off the darkness on your eyes.

In the grace of prayer,
The peace angel will hover with my soul
And shall efface the tanks' tracks
From the wheat stalk dream.
    And say the food grace,
With Golgotha loaves,
And the food of your noble children.
I shall declare your glory
For ten thousand years,
And ten thousand years,
And ten thousand years,
And then declare:
In the beginning was Ariha.
It remained Ariha.
And will stay Ariha.
Will stay, will stay, will stay.
Ariha.

Ramah, October 2010
(pp. 5–13)

Rap 8

Refrain from the curse evil,
Refrain from sedition and deception evil.
God on high is not your father's estate broker.
God on high is not a surveyor
At the office of "Israeli lands."
Your game is exposed.
Your box is uncovered,
Your black secrets box.
Your testimony is invalid,
From A to Z.
Did you come from the swamp of reeds,
Overridden by anaconda instincts?
Did you come from the depths of obscure sea,
With the culture of sharks?
Refrain from aggravation evil.
Be a human like humans.
This is a homeland, not a graveyard.
This is a home and not a coffin,
A home, not a coffin,
A home, a home, not a coffin.

Ramah, March 2012
(p. 34)

Clarity
A *Flock Poem: Selections*

Everything here is clear;
No dust or fog on a balcony
The dream predicament is clear,
With its undulations in the land of torment.
The ceremonies do not claim authority.
Clear . . . everything is clear,
As the clarity of mirage.
The alphabets are shining
In the elegies,
Shining in the songs,
In their double and triple tunes.
And I am clear above the earth,
And under the earth,
Between the parents' rue plant,
And the apple of knowledge.
Clear, everything here is clear,
Like the last line that will end the book
And there is no book.
Everything here is clear,
Like the obscurity of the homeland,
And the mingling of languages about an idea,
Scattered by madness winds,
And not saved by a reasonable site,
On the frontiers of time.
Clear. Everything here is clear.

And me. Who am I?
A simple Arab am I,
And love all nations,
Despite all the pain.
A simple Arab am I,

And want peace,
Despite what they heaped on my shoulders,
Provoked my wrist,
And inflamed my ankle.
A simple Arab am I, and love peace,
Despite the invaders' injustice,
The despots' tyranny,
The darkness's chaos.
A simple Arab am I.
My speech is the clarity of speech
A simple Arab am I,
My homeland is my own,
My residence is here,
My departure is here,
My resurrection is here.
And I
Have rocks on my back,
But it did not bow,
Did not bow, did not bow.
And I am clear.
Everything here is clear.

How can I touch any food
When millions are deprived of their bread,
Which they dip in their tears!
And millions sleep, on thorns,
In heat and cold.
Their tragedies are tents.
Their hopes are fasting!
How can I live calmly,
Enjoying prayer and a pure ablution,
And millions are subdued
By one refuge after another
How can I stand

All this madness, torment, burning!
All right
My body, burn,
And light the darkness of the roads,
And let everything here be clear,
Everything here is clear . . .

                                        (pp. 37, 46–49)

⌐

Regardless! There is no sitting down
With what was easy to get
When rising up!
Our village will take hold[1]
Of all storms from the early gust.
There will be much to say
About the pain in brief.
A swallow may not come,
The spring may be delayed,
But it will come, will come.
Regardless of the clouds, the night, the storms,
And our motionless clocks,
Or the rough roads round the slope.

⌐

It is possible I should confess
That I am a child of myths
At their height,
A twin of a pomegranate tree,
In a deeply ambiguous autumn
With no blossoms, and no rain.

---

1. "Our village" is what the poet means by his symbol of *wardatutuffahajar*. Literally it refers to the rose of apple stone, where *wardatu* is Arabic for "rose," *tuffah* is "apple," and *hajar* is stone. So the rose (spiritual beauty), the apple (sensual or physical enjoyment), and the stone (the constant truth) are all embodied in our village, or homeland.

It is possible I should confess
That drought is heavy,
But a pomegranate on Ramah slopes,
In the lap of Mount Haydar,
Has not lost its hope in fruit,
For a near feast,
Regardless
Of fear of what heaped by the wind dust
On the possible season of harvest.

I prepare myself for a new dream,
But the corroding body surprises me
With the malady from within.
Surprises me the soul fatigue
From its mortal weight
Here is the phantom of divide,
A day here, a night there.
But our homeland village
Sees in the heavy darkness
The angel wing, regardless
Of walking in its minefield.
Our homeland village
Weaves on its days' loom
A new scarf for Christ's wound,
The expected, future Christ,
Regardless!

There is a bit of fear and hunger,
If the cold should violate childhood
In a dark night,
Then pull the quilt over the sleeping child,
Regardless
Of fear in her dream.

And do not ignore the end.
There is no harm in caution
And overlooking.
I say to you: no escape,
Love the sunrise,
And do not ignore the magic
In what the sunset formulates.
Love life for us and all nations.
      For all nations.
Love the promises of noble peace,
And do not be deceived by wars.
Snows melt. All snows melt,
And a healthy meadow appears,
And the right really prevails,
By the right of steady, heavy, long struggle,
And love prevails. The sun prevails.
All roads will shrink
To the family olive tree feast,
And its virtuous branches,
And all humans will celebrate
The tree feast.
And we celebrate, regardless
Of the wind, fire, and the dropping banner
And its decisive historical moment.
I say to you with all my strong ailment,
And my weak voice,
The invaders' storms of woe
And oppressors' night
And their detachments do not frighten.
At the end we stay and keep.
Regardless.
We are the pedigree.
We are the pedigree of our homeland village.
We are the divine will and decree.

(pp. 67–71)

Equal are we
In bread, roses, love, and sin;
In desiring the wheat stalk,
That begot a song.
Equal we are, the people of my land,
     And I love you without election,
Without ballot, without adjustment.
I love you . . . by consensus.
Without question, without argument.
Your mountains are my head,
The shoulders of my sun
My heart, your mountain slopes,
My soul, your hills,
My lifetime, your plains and valleys.
I said I love you, by consensus,
Ignoring the rest.

We burden it with our loads,
Unaware, unconscious of its burdens,
By force we upturn its ways.
I have to say, I have to repeat,
Leave it alone!
Nature's flowers are nature's art
Not for funeral and wedding rites.
Oh, offspring of a woman called nature
Leave her alone!
Crocodile skins are crocodile home,
Not for bags and shoes.
Do not enter the court of sin.
Do not meddle with the deposit.
Do not lodge the ruins in the home.
     Leave it alone!

The foxes' fur is the foxes' warmth,
Not for handbags or covers.
Do not ride the wave of sin.
Do not kill the shade.
Do not feed the fire the meat of the trees,
Nor our homeland village rose.
Regardless!

(pp. 74–75)

I came out of the desert of old,
With a letter and a sword,
On the back of a naked horse.
I tamed the remote sky showers
With the secret of the poem,
Loyal to my sky magic,
And the purity of my father's clear sky.
I have the palm trees, the steeds,
The nights and good health,
And I realize I am returning to the desert,
With my dream
And my mother's prayers,
My hand is my lofty palm tree,
My heart is the chants
Of my kind olive tree.
Alive I return. Regardless!
    I return to the desert.
It has my beginning,
In it is my end,
From it is my second birth.

(p. 78)

And what do I love from God and His creatures?
I love what I don't love, and whom I don't love.

I hate my sudden hatred,
Every now and then.
I love the sparrows' prayers,
In the blue sky, after beautiful torment,
And the fever of poems at night,
My concealed night.
I love the beautiful call for prayer,
With its wonderful nature.
I love the peaceful prayer
In a peaceful retreat.
I love the ringing of the matins bells,
And the neighbor nun in her bashful steps,
Answering the greeting,
Regardless,
And greeting every passerby
In a shy and lucid voice.
I love the innocence of convent monks,
(From Tibet, spreading godliness to the Himalayas)
Through convent monks
Who love Buddha and the whole world.
I love the lovers from East and West.
I love the enemy
Who was taught by experience
How to become a genuine friend.
I love the readiness of firemen,
Before the raging of the fire,
And after the dying of the fire.
I love the loyalty of doctors and rescuers,
I love educators and laborers.
I love my childhood friends and classmates,
And those who shared with me,
The prisoner's care, and dream, and tobacco.
I love the one who bows,
To remove a stone,
A piece of bread,

Or a shred of cloth, from the road,
Regardless,
To secure for passages by,
Regardless,
Steps, in a clean, safe passage.
I love the well-brought-up boy
Who helps an old man
To cross from one platform to the other.

(pp. 81–83)

11

Collage 3 (2012)

Selections
Beirut, 2012

I play on the double flute
For my *Dabka* dance
On my night of celebration.
And here you are
Playing on your tank,
Hugging your tommy gun,
Haunted with depression.

(p. 12)

The dear enemy can do
Whatever he likes:
Pour bullets on my corpse.
And I will pour my blood
On his forehead,
And pour him my coffee.
If he likes to finish,
The mortal enemy can do.
I wanted what I desire
For him to end. But I said I will not end.
I am clear. . . . I said: I will not end.

(p. 15)

An armored vehicle is in the garden.
The roses shiver with horror.
A bomber bounces to shell
From a strange space.
And bounces, with grief
The butterfly wing.

(p. 20)

For thirty silver coins?
Jesus Christ, you were not cheap;
But Judas was the cheap one.
The thirty silver coins
Is the price of Judas,
Oh, my friend, Jesus Christ.

Ramah, March 2010
(p. 22)

My disappointment with your children
Was from the start,
And my regret is not extinguished yet
When my disappointment flared.
Oh, my nation
My revolt is still my revolt.

We have no more a passage
Between Baghdad and Cairo
We no longer have a passage, except
What the passports allow,
And the aeroplanes.

Do not think the autumn is mourning
With the trees' tears.
It is a call for the rain songs.

Between two fires I walk
On a thousand fires.

My steps on the fire will efface
A prison with a thousand walls.

Ramah, July 2010
(pp. 27–30)

We are still in the hard times'
Exhibition hall.
The Arab world cinema
Is still in its present scene
A nightmarish anxiety.
One of the horror films.

Do we have any hope?
Brothers, we are
A nation with no leader,
With no state,
With no capital,
Do we have any hope?

Ramah, September 2010
(p. 41)

All peoples' religions,
All races' rites,
Cannot be pardoned by a human's tear
Who is wronged, oppressed, or suffocated

(p. 55)

All right. I shall surrender to God,
What pleases Him, as it pleases Him.
But,

Caesar has no right with me
To surrender to him.

The vineyard that I planted,
With my hands,
How can its clusters be offered
To someone else,
And all the crop left to me
Is a sigh between the breaths
Of a flute?

Ramah, September 2011
(p. 68)

The rain is not asked
What did its waters irrigate.
The trees are not asked
Who gathered their fruits.
So, learn, learn,
My human brothers

Ramah, November 2011
(p. 75)

Drink your cup of coffee,
You, Cancer,
So I can read your luck
In the cup. Drink.

Ramah, January 11, 2012
(p. 85)

~ 12 ~

Collage 4 (2014)

In a popular ceremony held to sign this last collection,
the poet was rushed to the Safad Hospital in Palestine on
August 18, 2014. The malignant disease prevailed on the
poet's love of life, and he passed away one day later, on
August 19, 2014.

Selections
(Amman, Jordan, 2014)

"My pictures in the newspapers
Look like my pictures in the poems,"
Said a reader from a distant land.
I approached and shook hands with him,
And painted him a picture
In blood, of new letters.

(p. 56)

Will it be sweet and fair,
The love song we sing
For a dried rose?

(p. 7)

After my death, you will remember my life
  And the past will return on a future rhythm.
  In the land of the living I revived my death,
  And shall live in the world of the dead!

(p. 12)

O, summer, my last-year summer,
You were, how you were congested with medicines,
With tablets, serums, and chemicals,
And some serious talk,
About a morning with no evening . . .
O, summer, tell me (and be honest) will the autumn be
A scene of the fall of my light grey hair,
In the fall of my nakedness leaves,
And those of the trees?
Or will danger limits narrow down?

Will serious talk be too narrow
For the blast of my winds, and departure winds?
Let it be!
Here I am ready for departure,
In a morning cleaned
By a drizzle of the rain,
And a gentle, mild breeze.
Let autumn do what it likes.
Here I am ready for departure,
Not in a hurry, for I am fond of life.
I can see what it sees, though it thinks I do not see it,
I can see a ready appointment,
And I am ready . . . ready for departure.

(p. 47)

Outside the rose, the hedge and Arabian jasmine,
After our party,
After the departure of the guests, to the last reveler,
I realize now, how tired you are, tired.
Ah, my good wife,
My wife and life companion, mother of the sons.
You feel, and I know how you feel
When you see
The joy of sadness in my laugh.
You see in what you see
My agony and yearning
To a time passed, filling a healthy calendar,
And the hymns of our pure elation,
Of our happiness and that of our home and family,
Under the olive tree of abundant grace.
And now I realize how tired you are, tired,
Of my medicines, malady, doctor's examination
And fear of what is said of my health,
Of the rising temperature, every now and then.

You worry too much about my state, you worry
On my health, you stay up late
Like a mother on her child, you stay up.
Ah, my good wife
I do not like to talk about the dreadful moment . . .
A bell in the sand,
Whose resonance expired,
And was satisfied with the prayer of absence.
You stay well, my good wife.

(p. 50)

Our land is fertile,
And blessed
With palm trees, oil, wheat, figs,
And with enormous wealth.
But we are, O, my nation,
An arid nation.

(p. 55)

Two stars . . . and one song
And a final singer with a voice
Slaughtered, by an extinct nation.
A tear, two tears, a river of tears,
What is the use!
Ah, cold firebrand
In the waste of your extinguished fire,
In the waste of your lifeless corpses,
What is the use
Of a sky with no promising cloud!
Ah, you cruel setback, recoil, regression!

(p. 69)

The Last Poem He Wrote for His Grandson, Samih, the Son of Yasir

My share of time has become scanty,
    And malady stiffened, rashly violating.
Death approached, trifling with my torture:
    Take my hand, it could be soothing.
Then God's miracle shone as a baby,
    Filling the house with joy, and ambition.
O, my grandchild, thanks, and thanks a lot,
    You have renewed your grandparents' souls.
Your parents chose a pretty name for you;
    They overflowed with good taste, and revealing clarity.
In refined tenderness they embraced me,
    And gave you my name, a candid example.
It is a sweet, pleasant, and gentle name,
    Which became sweeter when you became Samih

Your Grandpa Samih

His Very Last Line of Poetry

Poetry lover, ask not what new poems I have,
    A smile by my grandson is the most beautiful poem.

> *With Collage 4, the poet had published seventy-eight col-*
> *lections of poetry, prose, and translations. There are four*
> *more works extant.*

Samih Al-Qasim was born on May 11, 1939 in Zarqa', Jordan, where his father was a captain in the Frontier Military Guard. His family moved to Rama, West Galilee, where they owned land. That was in the first year of World War II. His family is of the Durooz Muslims, his ancestors were Qurmuti Arabs, rebels from the Arabian Peninsula, and one of his forefathers came to Palestine to fight the Crusaders with Salahuddin. That man was called Khair, who settled at the foot of a mountain in the area which still carries his name. When Samih finished high school, the Israeli government tried to draft the Durooz Arabs, to join the Israeli army, but Samih led a group to resist that law; so he was put in prison, and condemned to hard labor. He took different jobs as a journalist, always writing poetry on Arab and Palestinian affairs. He was honoured by several international organizations and academies. His close association with Mahmood Darwish and their struggle for the common cause was phenomenal.

For about three years, Samih had been struggling with a malignant disease. On August 18, 2014, when the poet was signing his last collection of poetry, *Collage 4*, he was taken to Safad Hospital, where the disease prevailed over the poet's love of life only one day later.

Abdulwahid Lu'lu'a is an Iraqi retired university professor residing in Cambridge, United Kingdom, whose previous translations have won a range of literary prizes. He holds a PhD in English literature from Case Western Reserve. He has taught at many Arab universities, published twelve books in Arabic, and forty-two books in translation, all on literary subjects. His most recent book is *Shakespeare's Sonnets* (2013), Arabic translation and commentary.